PRACTICAL SOCIAL WORK

Series Editor: Jo Campling

BASW

Social work is at an important stage in its development. All professions must be responsive to changing social and economic conditions if they are to meet the needs of those they serve. This series focuses on sound practice and the specific contribution which social workers can make to the well-being of our society.

The British Association of Social Workers has always been conscious of its role in setting guidelines for practice and in seeking to raise professional standards. The conception of the Practical Social Work series arose from a survey of BASW members to discover where they, the practitioners in social work, felt there was the most need for new literature. The response was overwhelming and enthusiastic, and the result is a carefully planned, coherent series of books. The emphasis is firmly on practice set in a theoretical framework. The books will inform, stimulate and promote discussion, thus adding to the further development of skills and high professional standards. All the authors are practitioners and teachers of social work representing a wide variety of experience.

JO CAMPLING

A list of published titles in this series follows overleaf

PRACTICAL SOCIAL WORK

Robert Adams *Self-Help, Social Work and Empowerment*

David Anderson *Social Work and Mental Handicap*

James G. Barber *Beyond Casework*

Peter Beresford and Suzy Croft *Citizen Involvement: A Practical Guide for Change*

Suzy Braye and Michael Preston-Shoot *Practising Social Work Law*

Robert Brown, Stanley Bute and Peter Ford *Social Workers at Risk*

Alan Butler and Colin Pritchard *Social Work and Mental Illness*

Crescy Cannan, Lynne Berry and Karen Lyons *Social Work and Europe*

Roger Clough *Residential Work*

David M. Cooper and David Ball *Social Work and Child Abuse*

Veronica Coulshed *Management in Social Work*

Veronica Coulshed *Social Work Practice: An introduction (2nd edn)*

Paul Daniel and John Wheeler *Social Work and Local Politics*

Peter R. Day *Sociology in Social Work Practice*

Lena Dominelli *Anti-Racist Social Work: A Challenge for White Practitioners and Educators*

Celia Doyle *Working with Abused Children*

Angela Everitt, Pauline Hardiker, Jane Littlewood and Audrey Mullender *Applied Research for Better Practice*

Kathy Ford and Alan Jones *Student Supervision*

David Francis and Paul Henderson *Working with Rural Communities*

Michael D. A. Freeman *Children, their Families and the Law*

Alison Froggatt *Family Work with Elderly People*

Danya Glaser and Stephen Frosh *Child Sexual Abuse*

Bryan Glastonbury *Computers in Social Work*

Gill Gorell Barnes *Working with Families*

Cordelia Grimwood and Ruth Popplestone *Women, Management and Care*

Jalna Hanmer and Daphne Statham *Women and Social Work: Towards a Woman-Centred Practice*

Tony Jeffs and Mark Smith (eds) *Youth Work*

Michael Kerfoot and Alan Butler *Problems of Childhood and Adolescence*

Mary Marshall *Social Work with Old People (2nd edn)*

Paula Nicolson and Rowan Bayne *Applied Psychology for Social Workers (2nd edn)*

Kieran O'Hagan *Crisis Intervention in Social Services*

Michael Oliver *Social Work with Disabled People*

Joan Orme and Bryan Glastonbury *Care Management: Tasks and Workloads*

Lisa Parkinson *Separation, Divorce and Families*

Malcolm Payne *Social Care in the Community*

Malcolm Payne *Working in Teams*

John Pitts *Working with Young Offenders*

Michael Preston-Shoot *Effective Groupwork*

Carole R. Smith *Adoption and Fostering: Why and How*

Carole R. Smith *Social Work with the Dying and Bereaved*

Carole R. Smith, Marty T. Lane and Terry Walsh *Child Care and the Courts*

Gill Stewart and John Stewart *Social Work and Housing*

Neil Thompson *Anti-Discriminatory Practice*

Derek Tilbury *Working with Mental Illness*

Alan Twelvetrees *Community Work (2nd edn)*

Hilary Walker and Bill Beaumount (eds) *Working with Offenders*

Anti-Discriminatory Practice

Neil Thompson

MACMILLAN

First published 1993 by
THE MACMILLAN PRESS LTD
Houndmills, Basingstoke, Hampshire RG21 2XS
and London
Companies and representatives
throughout the world

ISBN 0–333–58433–3 hardcover
ISBN 0–333–58434–1 paperback

A catalogue record for this book is available
from the British Library.

Printed and bound in Great Britain by
Mackays of Chatham PLC, Chatham, Kent
Reprinted 1993

For Susan and Anna

Contents

vii

Preface

In writing this book I was motivated by my desire to make the basics of anti-discriminatory practice available to social work staff and students in a clear and accessible form. I recognised that it was an ambitious task – to cover so much ground in such a relatively short space. None the less, I felt it was important to try to provide a foundation for further study and practice even if this left a great deal unsaid – and even if much of what is said only scratches the surface. But the aim is not to provide a comprehensive analysis, for that would be hopelessly unrealistic. The aim, rather, is to provide an introductory overview which outlines the main themes, concepts and issues and offers some guidance as to how to tackle them.

Some readers may find this a frustrating text. Problems will be raised but not resolved, issues will be touched upon but not explored in depth. This is perhaps the price we have to pay for covering such a broad area within one short book. But if this frustration spurs the reader to read other texts, discuss the issues with colleagues and so on, then this frustration will be no bad thing.

Hopefully, there will be many other readers who will experience no such frustration but will, in its place, encounter the beginnings of a much clearer picture of anti-discriminatory practice and all this entails. And the emphasis must be on *beginnings* as this is very much an introductory text, but also, I hope, a stepping stone to future learning and practice developments in this vitally important area of social work.

In order to cover so many complex issues in one book it has been necessary to simplify matters in a number of places, I have relied on simplicity in order to tackle complexity. However, I have tried not to let this spill over into over-simplification. The subject matter is too important to allow this to add to the confusion that already exists for many people and in many quarters.

There is a fine line to be drawn between making complex issues accessible, on the one hand, and distorting them beyond recognition to fit into pre-existing frameworks on the other. I hope I have managed to avoid straying over that line.

The issues tackled in this text ultimately require a collective response but, as I see it, raised levels of awareness and understanding are a pre-condition for the development of such collective action. My hope is that this book can play a part in this process.

NEIL THOMPSON

Acknowledgements

In preparing this text I have had the support and assistance of a good many people. In particular I must express my gratitude to Susan Thompson for her unwavering support – moral, practical and intellectual – and her commitment to helping me see this project through. I have also benefited greatly from the advice and guidance of Jo Campling in her role as series editor.

I am grateful to the staff of the Social Services Research Library at Commerce House in Chester for their assistance in obtaining much of the background material I needed in preparing the text and for the friendly and helpful manner in which they provided that assistance.

For offering critical comments on aspects of the first draft of the manuscript, many points from which have been incorporated in this final draft, I am indebted to Professor Michael Oliver of Thames Polytechnic, Bob Maclaren of Cheshire Social Services, and Mary Langan and Tom Hulley of the Open University. I am also grateful to Tom Hulley for the models of mental impairment described in Chapter 7, as these are based on materials he prepared for an Open University summer school.

Any weaknesses, inaccuracies or inadequacies which remain are, of course, my own responsibility.

1

Introduction

During the late 1980s, social work education became increasingly aware of the impact of oppression and discrimination on clients and communities. There was a growing awareness and recognition of the relative neglect of such issues in traditional approaches to social work. For example, in 1989, the Central Council for Education and Training in Social Work (CCETSW) laid down its regulations and requirements for the newly formulated Diploma in Social Work (Dip.SW) and included these references to anti-discriminatory practice:

> Social workers need to be able to work in a society which is multi-racial and multi-cultural. CCETSW will therefore seek to ensure that students are prepared not only for ethnically sensitive practice but also to challenge institutional and other forms of racism . . . CCETSW will also seek to ensure that students are prepared to combat other forms of discrimination based on age, gender, sexual orientation, class, disability, culture or creed. (CCETSW, 1989, p. 10)

This emphasis on combating discrimination is part of the process of establishing these issues as fundamental building blocks of qualifying training and subsequent practice. They are therefore seen as an essential part of the curriculum and the evaluation process.

This major development in social work education and training has also been reflected more broadly, to a certain extent at least, in social work policy, theory and practice (although it would be naïve not to acknowledge that much progress remains to be made in these respects). Anti-discriminatory practice is therefore featuring as a regular and high priority item on the social work agenda.

But it is not only students as new entrants to the profession who need a grounding in the theory and practice of anti-discriminatory social work. There remain very many practitioners, managers and trainers schooled in more traditional approaches to social welfare who want or need a better understanding of the theory base and practice implications of a social work based on the principles of anti-discrimination.

The primary aim of this book is to provide just such a grounding – for qualified staff, for those seeking qualification and for others with a general interest in modern social work, equal opportunities or related issues. The text seeks to clarify and to answer, in part at least, a number of important questions:

● What are the factors underlying discrimination and oppression, especially as they relate to social work theory and practice?
● What are the common concepts and issues across the various forms of discrimination – sexism, racism, ageism and so on? What are the key differences?
● Why is the development of anti-discriminatory practice so important?
● What are the necessary steps towards constructing a social work practice based on principles of anti-discrimination and equal opportunities?

Before beginning to tackle these questions, it would be helpful to outline the recent history of anti-discriminatory practice in order to be able to locate the analysis which follows within its historical context. I shall therefore sketch out some of the broad issues which have contributed to the current emphasis on anti-discriminatory practice in its various forms – anti-racism, anti-sexism and so on.

The historical background

The 1960s was a significant decade in a number of ways. Feminist thought took major steps forward (for example,

Friedan, 1968) and also gained major recognition in popular consciousness as the 'women's liberation movement'. Issues of equal rights and equality of opportunity for women became much more firmly established on the political agenda. At this stage, however, evidence of the impact of this on social work is rather hard to find.

Also during the 1960s issues of racial discrimination and the oppression of ethnic minorities achieved a higher political, media and public profile. This was particularly the case in the United States of America, especially in relation to such issues as segregated transport and schooling (Polenberg, 1980). A similar process of consciousness-raising also occurred in Britain, although, again, there is little evidence of the impact of this on social work.

Indeed, it was a decade characterised by the notion of 'consciousness-raising', in terms of both increased political radicalism and the emerging psychedelic drug culture. The radicalism was particularly apparent in the latter part of the 1960s, as evidenced by student protest, occupations and so on. It was a time of idealism and anti-establishment challenge of the status quo. This was accompanied by an increased emphasis on humanitarian values and liberation. It was a time in which progressive movements flourished and the breaking down of traditional barriers was being pursued on a large-scale.

The liberated, flower-power sixties also saw the growth in popularity of writers such as R. D. Laing (1965, 1967), who challenged orthodox notions of psychiatry and propounded a radical alternative – an alternative vision which did seep into social work thinking (Thompson, 1991a). This further contributed to a spirit of liberation and a cry for the removal of oppression (Cooper, 1968).

Whilst this process was underway in wider society, social work continued to be dominated by the influence of psychodynamics, although the beginnings of a sociological approach were starting to become evident (Leonard, 1966). Rojek *et al.* (1988) write of:

> the deep influence of psychoanalytical thought with a focus on the relationship to the external world and the ego reactions to the

drives of the id and the demands of the super-ego. Psychoanalytic ideas were seen as the only effective method of altering personality structure; and insight at that time was seen as primary goal and major strategy of intervention. (p. 21)

The grip of psychodynamic influence was indeed strong, but was already beginning to yield, to a certain extent at least, to the wider focus of sociology, with its emphasis on social processes and institutions (Heraud, 1970). The 'sociological imagination' (Mills, 1970) was beginning to be recognised as a valuable approach to social work education and practice.

This 'imagination' was more than a widening of the focus to include social, as well as psychological, factors. It embraced a new emphasis, a more critical approach geared towards 'debunking' taken-for-granted assumptions (Berger, 1966) and questioning dominant views and values. Sullivan (1987) exemplifies this in relation to poverty:

> The worker . . . may have exploited a sociological imagination to question commonsense understandings of poverty and to perceive poverty's objective and subjective meanings. The result may be to lead him/her to a conceptualization of poor people as victims of a social system predicated on inequality. (p. 161)

The influence of sociological thinking had the effect of producing a more critical and socially and politically aware social work with a stronger emphasis on social structure, deprivation and inequality. The seeds of a radical social work were being sown.

The second half of the 1960s also saw the introduction of anti-discrimination legislation in Britain, for example, the Race Relations Acts of 1965 and 1968 (Lester and Bindman, 1972). These acts constituted at least a partial recognition of the discrimination experienced by black and ethnic minority people in, for example, employment and housing. They were an attempt to outlaw unfair treatment of people on racial/ethnic grounds, although, as many critics have pointed out, they amounted to a very limited and largely ineffectual attempt.

Solomos (1989) expresses condemnation of the functionalist emphasis in the race relations literature, with its implied goal of integration and assimilation. In this context, anti-discrimination laws can be seen as a 'mixed blessing' – on the one hand, a move in the right direction towards anti-racism, but on the other, a potentially oppressive policy premised on the denial or abandonment of cultural identity (assimilation). Solomos links this mixed blessing to the two different interest groups reflected in the legislation.

> Legislation is a compromise between demands of those who are worried about immigration and those worried about racial discrimination. (1989, p. 81)

The 1970s saw the introduction of further anti-discriminatory legislation – a further race relations act (1976) plus, in relation to gender discrimination, the Equal Pay Act 1970 and the Sex Discrimination Act 1975 (Beloff, 1976).

Again, as with the 1960s legislation, there has been much criticism of sex discrimination laws for failing to address the fundamental bases of discrimination. They were also criticised for being unduly complex and for having too many exceptions (Pannick, 1985).

These legislative changes were part of a liberal programme of reform. They were liberal in the sense that they sought to humanise or ameliorate the existing social system without calling for a radical change in the structures and social arrangements in which racism and sexism could be seen to operate. There was therefore a significant gap, both politically and conceptually, between the class focus of the radicals and the race and gender focus of the liberal reformers. Both sets of people were striving for a less oppressive society but were approaching the issues from different angles and with different long-term aims.

It was not surprising, therefore, that the school of radical social work which which began in the late 1960s but emerged in a more influential form in the mid- to late 1970s focused primarily on a class-based analysis (the critique of capitalism) and only tangentially covered issues of race and gender. For example, two of the key radical texts clearly display this pattern: Bailey and Brake (1975) is a collection of eight essays, but none relates primarily to race or gender (although one, Milligan, discusses what would today be referred to as 'heterosexism' – see Chapter 7 below); Brake and Bailey (1980) do, however, reflect some movement forward, and within their ten essays include one on feminism (Wilson) and one on racism (Husband).

Peter Leonard, in his Foreword to Dominelli and McLeod (1989) acknowledges the failure of earlier radical social work, premised on classical marxism, to take account of issues of gender and patriarchy. Issues of race/ethnicity and racism were similarly paid little or no attention. The critique of capitalism, a central plank of radical social work, necessarily hinged on notions of class conflict and exploitation. This was not to deny the oppression associated with race and gender; the problem was the lack of scope within the analysis to incorporate these concerns.

The emergence of radical social work drew attention to the structural and political context of social work and the key part played by concepts such as ideology, oppression and discrimination:

> In assessing their clients and delivering their services, social workers are undertaking a profoundly ideological task on behalf of the established structures: at the same time they are often trying to help clients to resist the most oppressive and discriminatory features of the welfare system. (Corrigan and Leonard, 1978, p. viii)

Radical social work was therefore premised on the following arguments (amongst others):

● Social workers need to recognise the sociopolitical context of the life experience of their clients and of their agency role and function;
● The dangers of social work practice contributing to and reinforcing oppression and discrimination must be recognised and guarded against; and
● Opportunities for emancipation of clients from oppressive and damaging circumstances should be seized upon as part of a project which alerts clients to the social and political basis of their problems and difficulties.

As we shall see below, these are also essential building blocks of anti-discriminatory practice.

Although radical social work achieved a higher profile in the mid- to late 1970s, there were elements of such an approach apparent before this time. Hearn (1982) sees its roots as extending back to the previous decade, to the 'protest and alternativism of the sixties' (p. 22). Simpkin (1989) is more specific in linking the movement to the political upheavals of 1968:

> The events of 1968 released an energy which manifested itself in a variety of social and cultural forms, one of which was a political activism which became more and more independent of the traditional parties. This consciousness was fed by a generalised sense of injustice which sought both inspiration and justification from the now burgeoning academic industry of social analysis. A growing acquaintance with the hypocrisy, injustice and repression which characterised the machinery of the state created a wider and more receptive audience for class-based doctrines of revolt. (Carter *et al.*, 1989, p. 160)

The radical social work of the 1970s was therefore a development of the emancipatory and progressive ethos of the 1960s, but linked specifically to class analysis and class struggle.

The increasing influence of sociology on the social work education curriculum had also no doubt made inroads into the traditional, psychologically-based infrastructure of social work theory and practice and thus paved the way for a more radical approach. But even this sociological influence was primarily class-based and lacked much of the breadth of other forms of sociology that also noted the relevance of gender, race, religion and so on. In short, despite the impact of sociology, the radical social work of the 1970s centred on the critique of capitalism but with only the faint beginnings of a critique of patriarchy and imperialism.

Simpkin (1989) relates this to the specific political tactic, dating from 1974, of concentrating on trade-unionism and class struggle which entailed 'downgrading' issues of women's and gay rights (ibid., p. 166). For this reason, amongst others, radical social work remained locked into class without acknowledging the role of other social divisions in the oppression and dehumanisation of social work's clients.

It was only in the 1980s that the primacy of class was seriously challenged and issues of gender and race began to be taken firmly on board by radical social work – by this time a much weakened movement made distinctly less popular by the emergence, and dominance, of New Right ideology with its promotion of individualism and its mistrust of all forms of collectivism.

The influence of feminism in sociology was now beginning to extend to social policy in general and social work in particular. A number of key anti-sexist texts became available – including Ungerson (1985) and Pascall (1986) on social policy; Brook and Davis (1985) on the family and welfare; and Hanmer and Statham (1988) and Dominelli and McLeod (1989) on social work practice from a feminist perspective.

For a profession whose basic-grade workforce and clientele are both predominantly female and in which a major focus is on 'the family', the feminist plea for an anti-sexist approach to social work is long overdue. It is an indication of the strength and dominance of patriarchal ideas that the 'gendered' nature of social work should have been neglected for so long.

The development of interest in issues of race and racism within sociology has also permeated into social work and the thrust towards an anti-racist social work has steadily gained ground. The Association of Black Social Workers and Allied Professionals (ABSWAP) was formed in 1983 and has consistently argued for more black social workers, a greater understanding of the nature and impact of racism, and a firmer commitment to the development of anti-racist social work.

But this is only one example of the increased recognition of racism as a social problem and the dangers of an uninformed social work practice reinforcing its effects. As with anti-sexism, the 1980s saw the publication of a number of key texts which have played a part in the strengthening of the anti-racist movement. Dominelli (1988) is a useful introduction to anti-racist social work in general, whilst Coombe and Little (1986) adopt a training perspective. Ely and Denney (1987) and Rooney (1987) are also helpful texts; Ahmad (1990) provides a very useful text with a clear practice focus, as does the set of readings produced by CCETSW (CD Project Steering Group, 1991); Ahmed *et al.* (1986) address child care issues; Fernando (1989), mental health; and Norman (1985), old age. Also, Bhat *et al.* (1988) is a useful information source on demography and related issues.

A further aspect of the historical development of anti-discriminatory practice is the movement away from an individualistic, pathological approach to disability towards a social model which takes account of the wider social context in which disability is experienced and indeed constructed (see the discussions in Chapter 6).

Radical social work has therefore taken on wider issues of race and gender and, albeit to a lesser extent, age, disability and sexual orientation. However, as these become more established, they also became less radical – they become part of the establishment framework. This is an example of the reform versus revolution dilemma (Pritchard and Taylor, 1978) in which piecemeal reformist improvements, whilst welcome in their own right, may reduce the impetus towards more radical solutions. Jones and Novak (1980) argue that social reformers have bolstered ruling-class interests by introducing measures which, though reducing discontent, inhibit or obstruct radical social change. Whether anti-discriminatory practice can keep in touch with its radical roots or whether its potential for social change will become diluted (by its incorporation into mainstream policy and practice) remains an open question. We have now reached the stage where greater consciousness of oppression and discrimination have been achieved, as is reflected in the range of literature and training courses available, the development of equal opportunities policies (in embryo form at least) and the regulations relating to social work qualifying courses (CCETSW, 1989, 1991a).

Anti-discriminatory practice is now firmly on the agenda, although much confusion still remains in relation to its basic premises, its theory base and the principles of good practice. Having sketched out the historical background we can now move on to address some of these issues. First, however, we need to pose the fundamental question: why is anti-discriminatory practice so important?

Good practice is anti-discriminatory practice

Social workers can be seen as mediators between clients and the wider state apparatus. This position of 'mediator' is a crucial one as it means that social workers are in a pivotal position in terms of the relationship between the state and its citizens.

The relationship is a double-edged one, consisting of elements of care and control, both potential empowerment and potential oppression. Which aspect is to the fore, which element or tendency is reinforced depends largely on the actions of the social workers concerned. Peter Leonard (1975) captures this point in relation to class and capitalism, although much the same can be said of gender and patriarchy, race and imperialism and so on:

> In capitalist society, social work operates as part of a social-welfare system which is located at the centre of the contradictions arising from the dehumanising consequences of capitalist economic production. Social workers, although situated in a largely oppressive organisational and professional context, have the potential for recognising these contradictions and, through working at the point of interaction between people and their social environment, of helping to increase the control by people over economic and political structures. (Bailey and Brake, 1975, p. 55)

What this suggests, in effect, is that there can be no safe middle ground, no liberal compromise. Social work is not, as Halmos (1965) would have it, a matter of the personal detached from the political (Pearson, 1975b).

As I have argued previously (Thompson, 1992a):

> There is no middle ground; intervention either adds to oppression (or at least condones it) or goes some small way towards easing or breaking such oppression. In this respect, the political slogan, 'If you're not part of the solution, you must be part of the problem' is particularly accurate.
>
>   An awareness of the sociopolitical context is necessary in order to prevent becoming (or remaining) part of the problem. (pp. 169–70)

In short, a social work practice which does not take account of oppression and discrimination cannot be seen as good practice, no matter how high its standards may be in other respects. For example, a social work intervention with a disabled person which fails to recognise the marginalised position of disabled people in society runs the risk of providing the client with more of a disservice than a service (see Chapter 6 below).

I hope this principle – that good practice must be anti-discriminatory practice – will become more clearly and firmly established in the chapters that follow.

Multiple oppressions

There are many texts available which concentrate on a particular aspect of anti-discriminatory practice, whether this be anti-racism, anti-ageism and so on. This book, however, is not intended simply as an introduction to each of the discrete areas. There is an underlying thread of 'multiple oppression', the interaction of various sources and forms of oppression.

Oppression and discrimination are presented as aspects of the divisive nature of social structure – reflections of the social divisions of class, race, gender, age, disability and sexual orientation. These are dimensions of our social location and so we need to understand them as a whole – as facets of an overall edifice of power and dominance rather than separate or discrete entities.

At the Critical Social Policy conference on 'Citizenship and Welfare' (London, March 1991), two of the papers presented made reference to the need for an integrated approach, a framework that recognises the interactions of multiple oppressions. Amina Mama stressed the need for a 'politically holistic approach – a politics of alliance' based on an integrated analysis. Race, class, gender and so on are separated out for analytical purposes but they are not entirely separate processes; they occur simultaneously and affect people in combination. They are related dimensions of our complex existence rather than discrete entities.

Fiona Williams expressed similar views in advocating a wider analysis which goes beyond class, race and gender to include marginalisation on the grounds of age, disability and sexuality. She argued for a theoretical approach which recognises diversities in patterns of power and inequality, but one which does not fall into the trap of establishing a 'hierarchy of oppressions'. The task, she affirmed, is to relate the diversity and differences between forms of oppression, on the one hand, to a need for an anti-oppression alliance on the other (see also Williams, 1992).

Both Mama and Williams are advocating an *integrated* approach, one which recognises the reality of multiple oppressions but which seeks to concentrate on the commonalities and shared aspects of alienation, marginalisation and discrimination. In short, political energies should be directed towards fighting oppression in its various forms rather than in-fighting between different anti-discrimination interest groups.

This is, of course, easier said than done, but the argument does have implications for social work policy and practice, as each of the later chapters will indicate. The notion of an integrated analysis is a central one to this book as my focus will be very clearly on the conception of anti-discriminatory practice as a unitary whole (rather than simply the sum total of anti-sexism plus anti-racism plus anti-ageism and so on). It has to be recognised that the combination of oppressions and their interaction is a complex, intricate and relatively under-researched area (Stuart, 1992; Morris, 1991; Williams, 1992) but one which none the less needs to be addressed.

 Oppression and discrimination are multifaceted phenomena and so it is important to gain an understanding of both the common themes across areas and the key differences between them.

Structure and outline

Chapter 2 examines the theoretical concepts and framework which underpin anti-discriminatory practice. The major themes will be explained and links with social work practice drawn in order to begin to build a bridge between theory and practice. Indeed, the need for a clear practice focus, illuminated by theory, will be a primary concern throughout the book. This chapter will also tackle the thorny issue of language. The topic will be approached from two angles; first, to understand the role played by language in constructing and reinforcing discrimination; and, second, to clarify the terminology used in this text, that is, to define the key terms and concepts.

This chapter sets the scene for the following analysis of the various forms of oppression and discrimination. This is achieved by explaining the common theory base which acts as a framework for understanding the complex issues discussed in ensuing chapters. Chapter 3 is the first of four chapters to explore a specific area of discrimination, in this case gender. The theory of patriarchy is explained and the steps towards an anti-sexist practice are sketched out. Chapters 4 to 6 follow a similar structure and pattern. Chapter 4 addresses issues of race/ethnicity and racism. Imperialist ideology and notions of cultural superiority are explored and rejected as a first step towards building a social work practice based on principles of anti-racism. In Chapter 5 the less publicised and less well established concept of ageism is the object of our attention. The issues of discrimination on the grounds of age are considered and a framework for developing anti-ageist practice is presented. Chapter 6 adopts a similar approach in exploring the marginalisation of disabled people. Discriminatory attitudes, policies, structures and practices are identified and the oppression inherent in catering only for the able-bodied majority is recognised as a target for change.

In addition to these four main areas, there exist a number of other forms of oppression and discrimination. These are the subject matter of Chapter 7, in which attention is paid to discrimination on the grounds of sexual orientation (heterosexism), culture and language, religion and so on.

Chapter 8 is the concluding chapter. It summarises the main themes and issues covered and examines possible ways forward. The focus here is on the need to evaluate critically one's own practice. This is necessary, as was suggested above, to ensure that social work is part of the solution rather than part of the problem.

2

The Theory Base

Social work theory derives from a wide range of sources although, traditionally, the social work literature owes much to social science thinking. In particular, the theory base outlined here draws heavily on sociology and social psychology.

This is not, of course, primarily a theoretical text – the major focus is on anti-discriminatory *practice*. But an understanding of the underlying conceptual framework, and the themes and concepts of which it consists, *is* necessary to ensure that such practice is based on intelligent and informed debate, rather than dogma, fad or ignorance.

I shall therefore present an exposition of some of the key themes and issues, and sketch out some of the linkages between the theoretical concepts and the social work concerns they are intended to illuminate. This will, of course, be a far from comprehensive account – a text of this size devoted entirely to such issues would still barely do justice to the complexity and scope of the subject matter. This chapter is therefore very much an *introductory* exploration of the theory base. It is a beginning which will, I hope, have the effect of both equipping and motivating the reader to build on these foundations through further reading, discussion and above all, putting such theory into practice.

Social divisions and social structure

Societies are not, of course, simply amorphous masses of people. A society is characterised by differentiation – people

14

are categorised according to social divisions such as class and gender. These divisions then form the basis of the social structure – the 'network' of social relationships, institutions and groupings – which plays such an important role in the distribution of power, status and opportunities.

People can be 'located' within the social structure in terms of the intersection of different social divisions (Berger, 1966). That is, who we are depends on how and where we fit into society. And this, in turn, depends on the complex web of social divisions or social 'strata' (hence the term 'stratification'). These strata are many and varied but the emphasis here will be on the major social divisions, those of class (Jones, 1983); gender (Mayes, 1986); race/ethnicity (Rex, 1986); age (Phillipson and Walker, 1986); and differential ability – able-bodied/disabled (Oliver, 1984). This is not to deny the importance or relevance of other social divisions such as sexual orientation, creed or linguistic group. It is simply a matter of having to restrict the scope of the analysis for reasons of space.

Let us look briefly at each of these dimensions of the social structure before considering their significance for social work.

Class

There is a major debate within sociology concerning the definition of class. There are those who, following Karl Marx, define class in relation to ownership or control of the means of production (specifically, the means of producing wealth – land, factories, machinery and so on). There are others, who, following Max Weber, relate class to 'relations of exchange' (that is, buying power) rather than relations of production (see Giddens, 1971, for a fuller discussion of these issues).

Within social work, the term tends to be used loosely, in a broadly Weberian sense, to indicate different levels of economic power. Low class position (equals low economic power due to low pay or reliance on benefits) is associated with poverty (Walker and Walker, 1987), poor quality housing (Donnison and Ungerson, 1982), poor health (Townsend and Davidson, 1982) and a general lack of opportunity.

Gender

There are distinct and relatively fixed biological differences between men and women. These are *sex* differences. However, when we ascribe particular social significance to these differences, and allot roles accordingly, they become *gender* differences. That is, it becomes a matter of social construction rather than biological determination.

Boys and girls are socialised into differential patterns of behaviour, interaction, thought, language and emotional response. Different roles are assigned according to gender, and so differential sets of expectations are established. These expectations are constantly reinforced through social interaction and the influence of the media, the education system and so on.

Where people deviate from these gender expectations, sanctions are applied – boys who stray into feminine territory are labelled 'cissy' or 'effeminate', whilst girls who transgress are seen as 'butch' or a 'tomboy'. These childhood patterns become deeply ingrained and persist through to adulthood.

Gender expectations can also produce a situation whereby the same characteristic can be interpreted differently according to whether it applies to a man or a woman. For example, assertiveness in men can be seen as strength of character whereas in women it can be seen as bossiness. The cycle is complete when biological sex differences are used to justify or 'legitimate' the inequalities inherent in social differences based on gender. This is an important point and so this link between the biological and the social will feature again below in the discussion of ideology.

Race/ethnicity

'Race', like sex, is often assumed to be a biological matter, but Pilkington (1984) argues that race is not a biological category; it does not adequately account for the distribution of genes within and between population groups. He goes so far as to say:

> For not only are we unable to account for the differences in the role of, say, black and white people in biological terms, but

serious doubt can be cast on whether it is meaningful to talk of race at all in a biological sense. (p. 3)

It is partly for this reason that the term 'race' often has the word 'ethnicity' attached to it – to emphasise that it refers to a social grouping rather than a biological one. That is, it is the equivalent of gender rather than sex. For the same reason many authors consistently place inverted commas around the word ('race') in order to indicate that it is not being used in its literal, biological sense.

Race is therefore a socially constructed way of categorising people on the basis of *assumed* biological differences. As with socially constructed gender distinctions the notion of race entails:

- *Inherent inequalities*. Racial categorisation involves not only *difference* but also implies relations of superiority/ inferiority. This is the basis of *racism* (see Chapter 4).
- *Biological legitimation*. The biological aspect of this social division is used as a justification for discrimination and inequality.

Age

The problems associated with sexism and racism have long been recognised and are relatively well documented. Discrimination on the grounds of age, or 'ageism', as it has become known (Butler, 1975) is a relatively new addition to anti-discriminatory discourse. Fennell *et al.* (1988) define ageism as follows: 'Ageism means unwarranted application of negative stereotypes to older people' (p. 97). As we shall see in Chapter 5, old age is strongly associated with notions of frailty, mental and physical debility and dependency. This association is greatly exaggerated by common (mis)conceptions about the nature of old age and the incidence of problems. This tendency to devalue older people and over-emphasise the negative aspects of later life is characteristic of ageism. The distribution of power, status and opportunities is therefore dependent upon not only class, race and gender but also upon age. Age is therefore an important social division, a significant dimension of the social structure. The main focus of anti-ageism is old age but when we consider that very similar issues apply to children, the impact of ageism takes on additional significance.

Disability

Disability is a concept which distinguishes a certain propor-tion of the population (those with some degree of physical impairment) from the 'able-bodied' majority. Again, this is not simply a biological/physiological matter; it has major social implications.

By defining disability as primarily a physiological matter, the issues are personalised and individualised. In this way, the social and political dimensions are overlooked. This leads Oliver (1989a) to comment:

> The growth of the disabled people's movement and, especially its redefinition of the problem as social oppression has given rise to the concept of disablism which is inherent within the individual model of disability. (Carter *et al.*, 1989, p. 192)

Thus it is argued that traditional, individualised approaches to disability mask the inherent marginalisation and dehuma-nisation involved in attitudes and policies in relation to people with disabilities. Once again, the biological level is used as a means of legitimating unequal power relations at the social and political levels. Disablism is the term used to describe the oppression and discrimination implicit in this situation – the social division of disability.

The psychodynamic focus of traditional social work has been criticised for its failure to take account of the social dimension. From this critique systems theory developed with its explicit emphasis on social systems. This, in turn, has been criticised for ignoring the importance of conflict, structure and social divisions. Social work theory has now progressed to a level of sophistication at which the part played by social divisions and social structure is receiving increasing attention. However, what is needed is a framework or model which will enable us to develop a clearer understanding of how the problems social workers and their clients face can be located in this wider, structural context. The PCS model that I shall explain below can, I hope, take us some way towards this.

The PCS model

In order to understand how inequalities and discrimination feature in the social circumstances of clients, and in the interactions between clients and the welfare state, it is helpful to analyse the situation in terms of three levels. These three levels (*P*, *C* and *S*) are closely interlinked and constantly interact with one another (see Figure 2.1). *P* refers to the *personal* or *psychological*; it is the individual level of thoughts, feelings, attitudes and actions. It also refers to *practice*, individual workers interacting with individual clients, and *prejudice*, the inflexibility of mind which stands in the way of fair and non-judgemental practice. *C* refers to the *cultural*

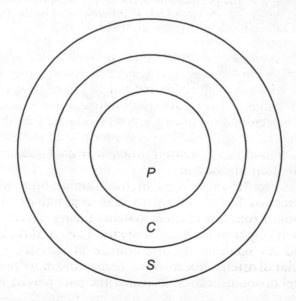

Figure   2.1

level of shared ways of seeing, thinking and doing. It relates to the *commonalities* – values and patterns of thought and behaviour, an assumed *consensus* about what is right and what is normal; it produces *conformity* to social norms and *comic* humour acts as a vehicle for transmitting and reinforcing this culture. *S* refers to the *structural* level, the network of *social divisions*; it also relates to the ways in which oppression and discrimination are institutionalised and thus '*sewn in*' to the fabric of society. It denotes the wider level of *social forces*, the *sociopolitical* dimension of interlocking patterns of power and influence.

The *P* level is, as Figure 2.1 illustrates, embedded within the cultural, or *C* level. Our thoughts, actions, attitudes and feelings are to a certain extent unique and individualised but we must also recognise the powerful role of culture in forming our opinions, guiding our actions and so on.

The *C* level represents the interests and the influence of society as reflected in the social values and cultural norms we internalise via the process of socialisation. Peter Berger (1966) captures this point well:

> Only an understanding of internalisation makes sense of the incredible fact that most external controls work most of the time for most of the people in a society. Society not only controls our movements, but shapes our identity, our thoughts and our emotions. The structures of society become the structure of our own consciousness. Society does not stop at the surface of our skins. Society penetrates us as much as it envelops us. (p. 140)

This passage is particularly relevant to the cultural influence of forms of discrimination on individual consciousness. It lays the foundations for understanding sexism, racism, ageism and disablism not simply as personal prejudice (the *P* level) but, more realistically, the discriminatory and oppressive culture base manifesting itself in and through individual thought and action (or '*praxis*'). It is therefore a more complex situation involving the interaction of the *P* and *C* levels.

Humour is an example of how a discriminatory culture can subtly but powerfully influence individual praxis. For example, racist jokes can be seen as a vehicle for reinforcing and legitimating notions of racial superiority. The fact that humour is so highly valued as a social quality means that it is both a highly potent influence and relatively well defended from attack. Comments such as 'it's only a joke' or 'it's only a bit of fun' act as effective defences and help to maintain the discriminatory power of humour. This is not to say that humour is necessarily discriminatory – far from it – but where it does have oppressive potential we need to be wary of allowing ourselves to be seduced by it.

To say that the P level is embedded within the C level is not to suggest the thoughts and actions of individuals are simply a 'reflection' of society or culture. The PCS model is not a deterministic one. It does not imply that culture 'causes' praxis but rather that individual behaviour has to be understood in the wider social and cultural context.

But even this cultural context needs to be understood in terms of a wider context – the structural. That is, the C level is embedded within the S level. It is no coincidence that we have the cultural and social formations that currently exist. These owe much to the structure of society – the interlocking matrix of social divisions and the power relations which maintain them. To understand the C level we need to relate it to the S level, the structure of society.

Marx argued that the economic base or 'infrastructure' conditions the 'superstructure', that is, the political, social and cultural aspects (the C level). This is an argument about *class*, the class conflict in the economic base of capitalism. But, as was argued in Chapter 1, class is not the only structural dimension that merits our attention.

Feminists have convincingly argued the case for recognising the importance of gender in mapping out the social structure, whilst the anti-racist movement has built on the foundations of a plea for understanding the racially-structured nature of modern Western societies. These topics will be discussed further in Chapters 3 and 4 respectively. The significance of age and disability as relevant dimensions of the social structure is increasingly being recognised too, as some of the discussions in this text will, I hope, confirm.

Marx's analysis does not, therefore, take us far enough but it is none the less a useful beginning. Indeed, I would contend that it is a grave mistake to reject marxism – a case of throwing the baby out with the bath water. I shall return to this point in the concluding chapter.

PCS analysis shows the different levels at which discrimination operates and how these levels reinforce each other. What is also worth noting, however, is that the degree of control and impact a worker can have on tackling discrimination is also related to the three levels, as is shown in Figure 2.2.

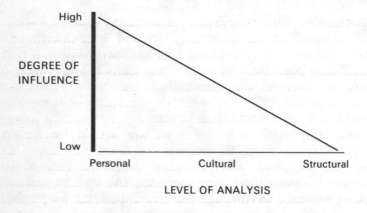

Figure   2.2

The further away one moves from the personal level the less impact an individual can have. It therefore becomes necessary to move beyond the personal level not only in terms of *understanding* discrimination but also in terms of *tackling* it. This involves individuals playing their part in collectively challenging the dominant discriminatory culture and ideology and, in so doing, playing at least a part in the undermining of the structures which support, and are supported by, that culture.

Structured inequalities and institutional oppression

One of the advantages of using the PCS model is that it shows the inadequacy of explanations which stop short at the individual level. For example, it is not enough to explain racism as a personal prejudice or the wicked misdeeds of a bigoted minority such as members of the National Front or the Ku Klux Klan. In fact, this more overt type of racial discrimination is referred to by many as 'racialism' (Nelson, 1990) to distinguish it from the wider concept of racism. As we shall see in Chapter 4, racism can be by omission rather than commission. It is not simply a matter of prejudicial beliefs.

If we accept that we live in a racist society (that is, a society that is geared to the white majority and thus discriminates against ethnic minorities) then it is not surprising that racist beliefs and practices will have been learned and 'taken on board' as parts of our personalities and what Berger and Luckmann (1967) call 'the taken-for-grantedness of everyday life'. Even if we are full of good intentions in relation to anti-discriminatory practice, unless we are actively seeking to eliminate racist thoughts and actions from our day-to-day dealings, they will 'filter through' from the culture and structure into which we were socialised and which constantly seek to influence us (through the media, political propaganda and so on.) It is in this sense that we cannot remain 'neutral'. As the political slogan would have it: 'if you're not part of the solution, you must be part of the problem'. That is, the tide of discrimination (the C and S levels) is so strong that unless we actively swim against it, it is more or less inevitable that we will be carried along with it.

I have used the example of racism but much the same can be said of the other forms of discrimination. For example, in terms of sexism, it is not simply a matter of a relatively small number of men who are overtly sexist or 'male chauvinist pigs'. Sexism subtly pervades our thoughts and actions and very often influences us in ways which we do not recognise until somebody points them out to us. (It is for this reason that 'Awareness Training' is an important prerequisite for anti-discriminatory practice – see Chapter 8).

Oppression and discrimination cannot be explained simply by reference to personal prejudice. Katz's (1978) notion of 'prejudice plus power' takes us in the right direction but ultimately confuses the issue more than it clarifies it (Sibeon, 1991a). Discrimination is a reflection (and a reinforcer) of structured inequalities. The fact that we live in such a highly stratified society means that inequalities are part and parcel of the social order – there are inevitably winners and losers. Again, this is not an individual matter, as such inequalities are 'sewn in' to the fabric of society – they underpin social order.

This introduces the notion of 'institutional oppression'. Oppression does not derive simply from individual praxis. It can be, and often is, built into structural and institutional patterns and organisational policies. Rooney (1987) gives a good example of how this operates. He describes how one local authority used to recruit its home-help staff by word of mouth. When vacancies arose, the existing (predominantly white) workforce would be asked to let people know of such vacancies. They would, of course, pass this information on to their (predominantly white) circle of friends, some of whom would then be recruited. Consequently, this form of recruitment systematically marginalised and excluded potential black staff, albeit perhaps unintentionally.

There are many aspects of social work which run this risk of institutional oppression (the inherent sexism of some forms of family therapy, for example – Dominelli, 1986). The concept is therefore an important part of the theory base of anti-discriminatory practice.

Ideology: the power of ideas

An ideology is a set of ideas which are associated with a particular set of social arrangements. The ideology has the effect of 'legitimating the status quo' and thus justifies, protects and reinforces those social arrangements and the power relationships inherent within them. For example, patriarchal ideology promotes traditional notions of the respective roles of men and women and strongly discourages any deviation from these. The power interests inherent in patriarchy are therefore well served by the ideology of patriarchy. In short, the ideas base safeguards the power base. In fact, this is what characterises ideology: the *power of ideas* operating in the interests of *power relations.* Hall (1986) captures this point as follows: 'Ideology helps to sustain social order because it is part and parcel of the power relations in society – it influences how power works and how conflict is expressed and managed' (p. 6). There are various ideologies at work in society but it tends to be the ideas of powerful groups which become dominant or, to quote the marxist dictum: 'The ideas of the ruling class are, in every age, the ruling ideas' (quoted in Bottomore and Rubel, 1963, p. 93). The ideologies of capitalism, patriarchy and imperialism are examples of such dominant ideologies.

Ideology can be seen to operate in a number of ways; that is, a number of 'ideological devices' can be identified. The setting up of 'norms' is an important part of this. An ideology will establish what is 'normal' and therefore, by extension, what is 'abnormal'. Ideology therefore defines deviance. 'Norm', however, is an ambiguous concept (Abbott and Sapsford, 1988, p. 77). It can refer to a *statistical* norm, a quantitative measure. For example, heterosexuality can be seen to be 'normal' in so far as the majority of people are heterosexual. However, 'norm' can also be used in an idealised sense to reflect what 'ought to be', that is, an *ideological* norm. It is a common ideological device for the two types of norm to be conflated – for an ideological norm to masquerade as a statistical norm. For example, the ideological norm of the nuclear family is often presented as if it were a statistical norm whereas, in fact, only 29 percent of households follow the nuclear family pattern (1985 figures, *Social Trends*, 1987).

Another very common primary device is that of presenting particular goals or values as 'natural'. The use of the term 'natural' is a very powerful way of gaining approval – it is a form of legitimation. To describe, for example, the traditional male role of breadwinner as 'natural' adds a false, pseudo-biological air of legitimacy. This is a particularly significant device in terms of the ideological justification of oppression. Racism is premised on the false notion of biological/natural racial categories, sexism on the reduction of social gender roles to biological sex roles. Similarly, disablism hinges on a medical (hence biological/natural) model of disability (Oliver,

1983) and there is an almost direct parallel here with ageism. Indeed, the masking of the economic and sociopolitical dimensions (of old age) under the guise of a biological or natural decline is an ideological device, parallel with the 'biology is destiny' axiom of sexism and the 'racial superiority' fallacy of imperialism (Thompson, 1992b).

The terms 'normal' and 'natural' both tend to have strong ideological overtones and so we should be very careful in using them, and sensitise ourselves to their use by other people. The logic of discrimination is perpetuated by ideology and so we should be very wary of these common ideological devices. Ideology refers to both the set of ideas which 'serve as weapons of social interests' (Berger and Luckmann, 1967, p. 18), that is the ideas themselves, *and* this very process of serving such interests – reinforcing the power base of the status quo. A significant part of this is the process of 'stereotyping'.

Righton (1990) introduces an important distinction between 'typifications' and 'stereotypes'. A typification is a set of characteristics and expectations we associate with a particular person, group or thing. It is a helpful way of simplifying the complexity of social reality and thus making sense of the world. It introduces and maintains a degree of stability and predictability. However, this helpful and constructive process can easily spill over into the much more harmful and destructive process of stereotyping:

> As long as we are prepared to regard the categories we construct as very rough generalisations, and to change them when new evidence shows them to be false, little harm can will ensue. The trouble comes when we become so emotionally attached to a particular typification that we experience any questioning of it as a threat to our self-esteem or sense of security, or as a challenge to the power we hold. We will then tend to cling desperately to that typification come what may, however strong the contradictory evidence. When this happens, the typification – now fixed and rigid – has become what we call a *stereotype*. (Righton, 1990, p. 11)

This is a matter of assumptions. In forming a typification we make certain assumptions – often ideological assumptions –

and, if we refuse to allow logic or evidence to challenge these, we run the risk of stereotyping as we are more prepared to reject evidence than we are to reject our own ideology.

This concept of stereotyping is a particularly important one in relation to discrimination and oppression. Dominance, inequality and injustice are often maintained by reference to stereotypes, for example of black people, of women, of old or disabled people. Stereotypes are therefore powerful tools of ideology and are thus significant obstacles to the development of anti-discriminatory practice.

In terms of the PCS model, ideology can be seen as the 'glue' which binds the levels together. It is ideology which acts as the vehicle of 'cultural transmission' between the C and P levels. Similarly, it is ideology which explains how the C level reflects, maintains and protects the S level by presenting social divisions as 'natural' and 'normal' and thus desirable. In short, the relationship between the levels is an *ideological* one, a reflection of the meeting point of the idea of power and the power of ideas.

Before leaving the topic of ideology, it is as well to point out that ideology is not an abstract force unconnected with human praxis. Indeed, it is in and through human action that ideology comes into being. It is part of the complex interplay of individual and wider social forces; it is the bridge between the external objective world of social circumstances and the internal subjective world of meaning. As such, it is an *existential* concept, a dimension of human existence rather than an abstract form in its own right (Thompson, 1992a).

The role of language

As ideology involves the communication of ideas, language is a central part of this process. It is therefore important to develop an understanding of the role of language in constructing and maintaining discrimination and oppression. It is a major subject in its own right and so the discussion here is necessarily selective. I shall focus on just two aspects, firstly the discriminatory nature of some language forms and secondly a clarification of the terminology used in constructing a basis for anti-discriminatory practice.

Many words and expressions have derogatory, or overtly insulting overtones whilst others are more subtle and less obvious in producing a discriminatory effect. For example, the British Sociological Association (BSA) have produced a set of guidelines on anti-sexist language which state: 'When reference to both sexes is intended, a large number of phrases use the word man or other masculine equivalents (e.g. "father") and a large number of nouns use the suffix "man", thereby excluding women from the picture we present of the world'. Thus the use of 'masculine' language to refer to both men and women contributes to the 'invisibility' of women and thereby facilitates the persistence of the gender imbalance in terms of status and power. This is 'exclusive' language, as it has the effect of excluding women.

Similarly, the BSA has produced a set of guidelines on anti-racist language, indicating which terms are appropriate and which are likely to have racist overtones. However, it is acknowledged that tackling these issues is difficult and far from straightforward:

> The issues are not always clear cut. There is disagreement as to whether some terms are acceptable or not and different political positions are aligned with different terms. Consequently, this guidance can only aim to promote an awareness of the issues in many instances rather than to prescribe or reinforce the use of particular terms.

The debate over terminology and racial discrimination will no doubt continue and it is likely that a definitive lexicon of anti-racism will remain elusive. The point is well made, however, that an awareness of, and sensitivity to, the oppressive and discriminatory potential of language must be a fundamental part of anti-discriminatory practice.

Language is also a key aspect of ageism. Fennell *et al.* (1988) comment on the importance of avoiding such terms as:

> 'the elderly', 'geriatrics' (as applied to people), 'the elderly mentally infirm', 'the old' or 'the confused' – but when we do have to generalise, we refer to 'elderly people', 'older people', 'ill

people', 'people in old age' or 'confused elderly people'. This is not to deny the physical realities of ageing, disability or dementia, but to try, linguistically, to remind ourselves constantly of human variety in the groups we are categorising and to underline the 'people status' (people like us, in other words) of elderly people as opposed to 'thing status' (objects inferior to us) of 'the elderly'. (pp. 7–8)

This passage captures well the depersonalisation and dehumanisation implicit in many of the common terms used to describe or refer to older people. It is a good example of how the *C* level (culture as embodied in language) has a significant impact on the *P* level of our day-to-day practice.

Bytheway (1985) makes a similar point in arguing that:

> popular attitudes and beliefs are based, to a considerable extent, upon the vocabularies and images found in currently available literature, and . . . there is in the production of literature a powerful regenerative element which serves to maintain dominant ideological perspectives. (p. 154)

Much the same can be said of the language of disability. Whilst depersonalised terms such as 'the elderly' are frowned upon by the anti-discriminatory movement, so too is the term 'the disabled'. A more appropriate term is 'disabled *people*' or 'people with disabilities'.

Webb (1989a) discusses the value of awareness training in drawing attention to the problematic nature of some of the commonly used terms: 'Courses enable participants to examine language and terminology. On the whole, words such as spastic and cripple are recognised as negative and derogatory' (p. 19). Language therefore needs to be used sensitively and critically in order to avoid negative connotations.

Davis (1988) points out that even officially defined terms can be discriminatory. For example, he distinguishes between the World Health Organisation (WHO, 1980) definitions of impairment and disability (with their individualistic emphasis) and those of The Union of the Physically Impaired Against Segregation (UPIAS) which underline the social nature of disability – the restrictions caused by *social organisation* rather than the impairment itself (UPIAS, 1976). This will be an important aspect of the discussions in Chapter 6.

Language therefore plays a significant part in the construction and maintenance of discriminatory and oppressive forms of practice. However, it has often been argued that the use of language is secondary to the good intentions of those using these terms. The argument goes: 'If people use such terms in good faith without intending any ill-will towards the groups concerned, surely it is petty to make an issue of the use of such language?'

This seems a reasonable argument on the surface, but when we look at it more closely the pitfalls become visible. The major point we need to recognise is that language is not simply a reflection of oppression (and thus an innocuous route if paved with good intentions, it could be argued) but actually *constructs* such oppression). Michel Foucault uses the term 'discourse' to refer to the way in which language and other forms of communication act as the vehicle of social processes (see Foucault, 1977, 1979). For example, medical discourse not only reflects the power of the medical profession, it also actively contributes to constructing, re-enacting and thus perpetuating such power.

Discriminatory language therefore both reflects the discriminatory culture and social structure in which we live, and also contributes to the continuance of such discrimination. Language is not a passive receptacle; it is an active encounter with the social world. Freire (1972) draws a similar conclusion:

> Human existence cannot be silent, nor can it be nourished by false words, but only by true words, with which men transform the world. To exist, humanly, is to *name* the world, to change it. Once named, the world reappears to the namers as a problem and requires of them a new *naming*. (pp. 60–1)

Language is part of the social world; indeed, it is one of the bridges between the personal and the social and, as such, it cannot be neutral. The language we use either reinforces discrimination through constructing it as 'normal' or contributes, in some small way at least, to undermining the continuance of a discriminatory discourse.

Rojek *et al.* (1988) also stress the importance of language and its discriminatory potential when they argue that: 'the language which social workers are trained to use in order to free clients very often has the effect of imprisoning them anew' (p. 1). This further underlines the need for a sensitivity to language and a critical approach to the forms of communication we commonly use. Indeed, it is largely for this reason that we shall now move on to clarify some of the key terms used in current attempts to promote anti-discriminatory practice.

This is not intended as a glossary and is far from comprehensive in its coverage. It will, however, hopefully lead to a clearer understanding of some of the central issues and thus make it easier to get to grips with the complexities of this intricate and thorny subject.

Discrimination

Unfair or unequal treatment of individuals or groups; prejudicial behaviour acting against the interests of those people who characteristically tend to belong to relatively powerless groups within the social structure (women, ethnic minorities, old or disabled people and members of the working class in general). Discrimination is therefore a matter of social formation as well as individual/group behaviour or praxis.

Oppression

Inhuman or degrading treatment of individuals or groups; hardship and injustice brought about by the dominance of one group over another; the negative and demeaning exercise of power. Oppression often involves disregarding the rights of an individual or group and is thus a denial of citizenship.

Anti-discriminatory practice

An approach to social work practice which seeks to reduce, undermine or eliminate discrimination and oppression, specifically in terms of challenging sexism, racism, ageism and disablism (these terms will be defined in subsequent chapters) and other forms of discrimination encountered in social work. Social workers occupy positions of power and influence, and so there is considerable scope for discrimination and oppression, whether this is intentional or by default. Anti-discriminatory practice is an attempt to eradicate discrimination from our own practice and challenge it in the practice of others and the institutional structures in which we operate.

Equal opportunities

A generic term for various forms of anti-discrimination, particularly with reference to employment-related issues – recruitment, promotion and so on. Implicit in the concept is the notion of *disadvantage* and the need to guard against it – by avoiding disadvantaging certain people (for example, through restrictive employment practices) and by promoting greater access to employment, training and promotion opportunities for members of disadvantaged groups (affirmative action). Equality of opportunity is closely linked to the notion of anti-discrimination and the anti-discrimination legislation (discussed in Chapter 1) which underpins it.

Prejudice

An opinion or judgement formed without considering the relevant facts or arguments; a biased and intolerant attitude towards particular people or social groups; an opinion or attitude which is rigidly and irrationally maintained even in the face of strong contradictory evidence or in the persistent absence of supportive evidence; a rigid form of thinking based on stereotypes and discrimination. Although prejudice operates primarily at the *P* level, it is closely linked with and informed by the *C* and *S* levels. Prejudices do not occur at random but rather reflect particular social divisions and social processes.

Radical social work

An approach to social work which seeks to locate the problems experienced by clients in the wider social context of structured inequalities, poverty, inadequate amenities, discrimination and oppression. It sees social work as primarily a political venture, a *struggle* to humanise, as far as possible the oppressive circumstances to which clients are subject. It is premised on the key notion of *empowerment*, the process of giving greater power to clients in whatever ways possible – resources, education, political and self-awareness and so on.

Definitions can, of course, obscure as much as they clarify, but the discussions and analyses in subsequent chapters will continue to cast light on these six terms and related concepts and issues.

Commonalities and differences

There are many common themes across the various forms of oppression. These include:

● prejudice and stereotypes;
● the dynamic interplay of the *P*, *C* and *S* levels;
● inequality and the denial of rights;
● power relations; and
● ideological legitimation based on biology.

There are also a number of others which have not been discussed here. For example, the concept of 'hegemony' is applicable across the board. This refers to the dominance of one group over another, or over a range of groups. One group, or 'social collectivity' (for example, men, white people, able-bodied people) gain power, status, position, prestige or some other advantage at the expense of other, less socially favoured groups (for example, women, black or disabled people).

Hegemony is therefore closely linked to the notion of exploitation, although not necessarily in any deliberate or intentional sense. It is also closely linked with ideology, for it is often through the vehicle of ideology that hegemony operates. As Esland (1981) comments:

> Hegemony, or dominance, in society is reinforced and main-tained both through control of the agencies of control of the agencies of force (e.g. the army and the police) and through the production of ideas that embody and project social structure. It is this second aspect of dominance that sociologists are referring to in the concept of *ideology* . . . An essential element of these various systems of ideas and perspectives, which is integral to the concept of *ideology*, is that they are in various ways projections and embodiments of the *interests* of the groups that promote them. (p. 58)

Part of the ideological basis of hegemony is the idea of an 'outgroup', a group of people defined in negative terms and assigned an inferior status. This can be recognised as part of the process of discrimination and oppression and is thus a further commonality.

It is important that social workers are aware of the common threads and are able to respond to them accordingly – through resisting or weakening their influence and softening or preventing their impact. The commonalities are also an important part of avoiding the development of a divisive 'hierarchy of oppressions' discussed in Chapter 1. Understanding the common themes is a major aspect of fighting the common enemies, those of discrimination and oppression. However, there are also significant differences between the multiple forms of oppression. It would be a mistake, both analytically and tactically, to concentrate exclusively on the commonalities without paying due heed to the important differences.

It is beyond the scope of this book to give a detailed and thorough exposition of the differences and so I shall restrict myself to a small selection by way of illustration of the wider field. Race and gender issues can be contrasted with age and disability issues in at least two ways:

1. In the former cases the oppressed have recourse to the law whereas, in the latter two, in Britain at least, there is no equivalent anti-discrimination legislation.
2. The people affected by discrimination on the grounds of age or disability are subject to the dangers of 'medicalisation'. That is, old or disabled people are construed as 'ill' (and thus 'invalidated') (Laing, 1967; Laing and Cooper, 1971), in a way which women and black people are not.

There are also varying levels of publicity given to the areas and different levels of public awareness of the issues, both within social work in particular and within the wider community at large.

There are also differences in the ways in which racism and sexism are experienced and combated. For example, womanhood is not a totally homogeneous, undifferentiated entity (it intersects with class, race/ethnicity, age and so on). However, it is a much more homogeneous concept than that of race. There is, for example, no consensus as to which groups should be classified as 'black' – or 'Black' with a capital 'B' to emphasise that it is a political, rather than descriptive term (Williams, 1989, p. ix). The BSA guidelines on anti-racist language note, for example, that: 'some Asians in Britain object to the use of the word "black" being applied to them and some would argue that it also confuses a number of ethnic groups which should be treated separately'. There is a danger, however, of overemphasising the differences and we should be clear about the need to focus on the commonalities and thus the common steps that can be taken to challenge oppression and fight discrimination.

There is a danger in placing too much emphasis on the disparate elements of oppression and thus failing to see the links between, for example, racism and sexism (Mama, 1989a), sexism and ageism (Peace, 1986) and so on. We can fail to see the patterns and common threads and thereby miss an opportunity for moving forward together as part of a wider anti-discrimination movement. It should also be re-membered that the various oppressions are separated out for purposes of analysis and clarity of exposition but are, in fact, dimensions of the same existence. People do not feel oppressions in isolation but rather as different but related aspects of what Sartre called 'lived experience' ('*le vécu*', Sartre, 1975).

This is a point which is particularly worthy of note in relation to the following chapters, where the focus of attention falls on a particular form of oppression (beginning in Chapter 3, with sexism). The point again needs to be made that sexism, racism, ageism, disablism and so on are analytical categories and thus part of a wider and deeper social process (that of hegemony, social division and exploitation) rather than distinct and unrelated forms of discrimination. Although substantially different, quantitatively and qualitatively and in both a historical and contemporary sense, these forms of oppression share enough in common to justify a unified theoretical approach to tackle the relevant issues in each of these areas.

This chapter has contributed towards the task of establishing such a theory base. However, it would be naïve in the extreme to assume that the theoretical tools given here are sufficient for the task of developing a genuinely anti-discriminatory practice. This chapter, and indeed this book as a whole, can only be a beginning, a few relatively small, but none the less important steps in the right direction.

3

Gender and Sexism

Gender is a fundamental dimension of human experience, revealing an ever-present set of differences between men and women. As Simone de Beauvoir puts it:

> In truth, to go for a walk with one's eye open is enough to demonstrate that humanity is divided into two classes of individuals whose clothes, faces, bodies, smiles, gaits, interests and occupations are manifestly different. Perhaps these differences are superficial, perhaps they are destined to disappear. What is certain is that they do most obviously exist. (1972, pp. 14–15)

But it is not simply a matter of difference, of interesting and benign diversity. As Abercrombie and Warde (1988) suggest, issues of gender can no longer be 'subsumed under the "family" with its connotation of a happy haven of consensus' (p. 206). Instead, they argue, gender inequality now occupies a central place in sociological discussion.

This notion of 'not just different but unequal' introduces the concept of *sexism*, inequality, discrimination and oppression on the grounds of gender – in short, male hegemony. But what exactly is sexism? What are its constituent parts and what impact does it have on social work? These are important questions and open up a number of significant issues which can be seen as central to the theory and practice of social work. It is therefore important to clarify the basis and dimensions of sexism and it is with this task that we begin.

What is sexism?

Sexism has been defined as:

37

a deep-rooted, often unconscious system of beliefs, attitudes and institutions in which distinctions between people's intrinsic worth are made on the grounds of their sex and sexual roles. (Bullock and Stallybrass, 1977, p. 571)

The reference to 'beliefs, attitudes and institutions' indicates that sexism operates at all three levels: *P*, *C* and *S*. The beliefs and actions of individuals, the cultural values and norms and the institutional or structural patterns all tend to display an inherent bias against women producing a situation in which women:

● earn less than men and are more vulnerable to unemployment;
● tend to be concentrated in less prestigious and less secure forms of employment; do considerably more housework than men; and
● experience substantial inequalities in relation to housing, welfare benefits and health (see Abercrombie and Warde, 1988).

Sexism is closely linked to the concept of *patriarchy*, literally 'the law of the father'. Weber (1947) used this concept to refer to the dominance of men within the family. Its use, however, has been extended to refer to the dominance of men in general, as is reflected in the distribution of power in society. Millett (1971) captures this point well when she argues that: 'the military, industry, technology, universities, science, political office, and finance – in short, every avenue of power within the society, including the coercive force of the police, is entirely in male hands' (p. 25).

Sexism is therefore a set of beliefs, practices and institutional structures which reinforces, and is reinforced by, patriarchy. The two concepts are mutually supportive. In particular, patriarchal ideology promotes the traditional model of the family: the male breadwinner as provider, head of the household and defender of his territory; the wife and mother as nurturer and carer; and their dependent children who; they socialise into following in the footsteps of the appropriate role model – boys to grow up like daddy, girls to grow up like mummy.

In fact, the links between patriarchy and the nuclear family are so great that the term 'familial ideology' has been coined to refer to the ideas base which seeks to legitimate these social relations. Helen Lentell (1988) describes the concept in the following terms:

> Familial ideology in our society asserts that the co-resident nuclear family is a universal and desirable way to live, and that the prevailing sexual division of labour, in which the woman is housewife and mother and primarily located within the private world of the family and the man is the wage-earner and breadwinner located in the public world of work, is universal and normatively desirable. (p. 46)

From this she goes on to depict the family as: 'the ideological site in which gender differences are constructed' (ibid.). The emphasis on the nuclear family as being 'normal' thus defines other family forms as 'deviant' and undesirable. The pressure to conform to sex-appropriate roles within the patriarchal family is both a major part of the socialisation process and a significant aspect of sexism.

A further constituent part of sexism, as referred to above by Lentell, is that of the sexual division of labour. Work tasks, both within and outside the home, tend to follow a gender-specific pattern. Women tend to be involved primarily in the domestic sphere of housework and childcare (Oakley, 1974) whilst men are more closely associated with the public sphere of paid work. The allocation of pay, status, leisure time and other rewards shows a distinct bias in favour of men at the expense of women.

Rowbotham (1973) links this to capitalism and the marxist notion of men as *producers* (that is, workers producing material wealth) and women as *reproducers* (that is, child-bearers and nurturers of the workforce). Pascall (1986) draws important links between this marxist analysis and social policy. She bemoans the overemphasis on production and thus relative neglect of reproduction. She therefore argues for a greater understanding of the role of the family in the sexual division of labour: 'The family, the boundary between public and private life, relations between state and family – these need analysing and understanding in their own right' (p. 22).

In particular, there is a need for greater attention to be paid to the ways in which the Welfare State reinforces familial ideology and the sexism inherent within it. Pascall comments: 'And by supporting the breadwinner/dependant form of family, with the woman at home, social policy has played a part in controlling women, keeping them in the private sphere and out of public life' (ibid., p. 25). This is an important point and will be relevant to the discussions below of the inter-relationships between social policy, social work and sexism/patriarchy.

A further aspect of sexism relates specifically to sexuality and the implicit (or sometimes explicit) assumption that male sexuality is a strong and 'difficult to resist' force. This assumption is then often used, in part at least, to justify or excuse male aggression against women. Jeffrey Weeks (1986) refers to this as the 'Biological Imperative' and it is yet another example of a biological argument being used as a basis for legitimating social relations, power and dominance. Weeks comments:

> The idea that there are differences between peoples is not in itself dangerous. What is peculiar about sexuality is that certain differences have been seen as so fundamental that they become divisions and even antagonisms. At best, there is the argument that though men and women may be different they can still be equal. At worst, assumptions about the forceful nature of the sexual drive have been used to legitimize male domination over women. (p. 47)

This 'dominance' can be seen to go a step further and emerge as sexual violence. Hanmer and Saunders (1984) flag up the significant extent of violence against women, including rape and sexual assault. For a variety of reasons, including the less than helpful response of the law enforcement agencies, a major proportion of these incidents go unreported and do not therefore appear in the crime statistics (see also Mama (1989b) for a study which focuses particularly on the experiences of black women).

These issues are also relevant to our understanding of, and response to, child sexual abuse, as will become clear in the following section concerning the implications of sexism.

Patriarchy, then, is one of the *structural* dimensions of society that is strongly associated with the sexist culture which demeans and disempowers women and thus sows the seeds for the cultivation of *personal* prejudice in terms of both attitudes and behaviour. The taken-for-granted nature of sexism at an individual level thereby promotes and protects the patriarchal structure. Thus, sexist ideology keeps the wheel of oppression turning.

But what impact does this have on social work? In what ways does social work fit into this picture? It is these issues I shall now address.

The implications for social work

One of the major implications for social work is the need to rethink radically the male-dominated and masculine-orientated basis of traditional social work theory. As Langan (1985) puts it: 'Although most social work clients and most social workers are women, the theory and practice of social work reflect little appreciation of the important question of women's oppression' (p. 28). Sexism raises many issues for social workers seeking to develop anti-discriminatory practice. Whilst this text cannot address all of them, we can at least begin to explore some of them.

Social work operates at the boundaries of 'normality' and 'deviance' (Pearson, 1975b) and so it is important that we recognise that our conceptions of normality are 'gendered'. That is, we need to become sensitive to the gender issues involved in the notion of 'normal'. For example, the concept of a 'normal' family, as commonly used, is likely to be a patriarchal family; 'normal' childrearing practices are also gender-specific – when we speak of 'good-enough parenting', we are, more often than not, talking of 'good-enough mothering', father remaining relatively invisible (Hanmer and Statham, 1988; Hudson, 1989).

It is therefore an easy step from taking 'normality' for granted to reinforcing stereotypical expectations of men and women. Carlen and Worrall (1987) comment on the expectations of a 'normal' woman:

> Being a normal woman means coping, caring, nurturing and sacrificing self-interest to the needs of others. It also means being intuitively sensitive to those needs without them being actively spelt out. It means being *more than man*, in order to support and embrace Man. On the other hand, femininity is characterised by lack of control and dependence. Being a normal woman means needing protection . . . It means being childlike, incapable, fragile and capricious. It is being *less than man* in order to serve and defer to Man. (p. 3)

A clear implication for social workers, therefore, is the need to develop a *critical* approach which questions and challenges everyday assumptions and thereby gets underneath the ideological gloss of 'normality'.

The converse of this situation also applies. That is, not only can social work be seen to reinforce sexism if a critical approach is not adopted, but sexism can also be seen to be a major factor underpinning many of the problems social workers are asked to tackle. The discrimination and oppression inherent in sexism are, of course, not without cost to the women concerned.

Poverty is one example of this, as women have more restricted access to resources than men. This produces a situation which Hanmer and Statham (1988) refer to as the 'feminisation of poverty', as so many women are reliant upon either men or state benefits for financial support: women receive one tenth of the world's income, and own less than one per cent of the world's property. A related concept is that of 'secondary poverty', the fact that women, even in relatively financially secure households, are often starved of resources – the man of the household taking a disproportionate amount of the family income to follow his leisure interests or other pursuits (Barrett and McIntosh, 1980).

Glendinning (1987) makes a similar point when she argues that:

> women bear the burden of managing poverty on a day-to-day basis. Whether they live alone or with a partner, on benefits or low earnings, it is usually women who are responsible for making ends meet and for managing the debts which result when they don't. Indeed, the lower the household income, the more likely it is that this responsibility will rest with women. (p. 60)

The links between poverty and the problems social work clients experience have been clearly established and are well documented. The fact that women constitute the majority of social work clients (Howe, 1985; Langan, 1985) adds weight to the 'feminisation of poverty' thesis and also underlines the linkages between gender, oppression and social work.

Poverty has also been associated with mental illness, and with depression in particular. Depression is also significant in terms of gender: women are heavily over-represented as far as this disorder is concerned (Miles, 1987). This is relevant for social workers at two levels:

1. Specifically in terms of mental health social work and the significance of gender for this type of work; and
2. More generally in relation to a range of social work situations in which depression plays a part: childcare (including child protection); loss and grief; work with older people and so on.

Brown and Harris (1978) undertook a study of the incidence of depression in women and sought to uncover the underlying factors. They were surprised by the relatively high frequency of depression amongst women, especially in urban areas. A number of 'vulnerability factors' were identified, for example, a low level of intimacy with the husband/partner, and these factors, in turn, tend to lead to low self-esteem. The low self-esteem of many women therefore leaves them much more prone to depression.

But Brown and Harris emphasise that these are sociological factors, to do with the position of women in society, rather than being purely psychological. They comment that depression is not only relatively common but also:

> fundamentally related to social values since it arises in a context of hopelessness consequent upon the loss of important sources of reward or positive value. A woman's own social milieu and the broader social structure are critical because they influence the way in which she *thinks* about the world and thus the extent of this hopelessness; they determine what is valued, as well as what is lost and how often, and what resources she has to face the loss. (1978, p. 270)

Although Brown and Harris do not refer specifically to sexism, it is clear that the same issues are applicable. Indeed, the PCS model is highly compatible with their work – the psychological level being embedded within the wider social milieu and social structure.

Reference was made above to child protection work and gender issues can be seen to be relevant here too. Parton and Parton (1989) refer to the concept of 'dangerous *families*', but argue that, in reality, the focus is on 'dangerous *mothers*'. Mothers are seen to have primary responsibility for children (this is a key part of patriarchal ideology) and are therefore held responsible when things go wrong. Even when the mother herself is not the abuser, she is deemed to be culpable by virtue of the fact that she has failed to protect the child (Beagley, 1989). In this respect, child abuse can therefore be seen as a failure of motherhood. Hudson (1989) uses the term 'mother-blaming' to describe this process. She comments on the continuing tendency to ignore to some degree the role of fathers. Parenting is seen primarily as mothering. Poor parenting, neglect or abuse are therefore construed mainly as a failure on the part of women.

Despite the fact that the majority of sexual abuse cases involve male perpetrators, the focus remains on the role of the mother. It is her role to protect the child in general and this includes protection from a 'driven and uncontrollable' male sexuality (MacLeod and Saraga, 1988, quoted in Hudson, 1989). Implicit blame therefore tends to be attributed to the female's 'failure to protect' rather than the male's proclivity to abuse.

This situation is a clear example of the strength and depth of the influence of patriarchal ideology. Women are cast as primary carers and so, in situations of child abuse, they find themselves in a 'no-win' situation. If they are the abusers (and we shall discuss this below), they have failed as mothers and thus failed as people. Where it is the menfolk who are the abusers, the women have failed in their duty to protect (and, in the eyes of some, also failed to 'keep their man happy'). Men, by contrast, tend not to be charged with a failure to protect, and even where they are the perpetrator some allowance is often made for their behaviour, based on essentialist notions of male aggression and unrestrained sexuality being 'natural' (the 'Biological Imperative').

Physical abuse of children has often been described as an abuse of parental power, or the power of adults over children in general. In sexual abuse, the gender dimension is more apparent as the choice of a child as a sexual partner can be seen as an example of male sexuality as a form of power (Jeffries, 1984; and Ash, 1984) and sexual abuse as an abuse of such power. Indeed, Corby (1989) argues that it is only the efforts of feminists that have brought the problems of child sexual abuse to light, and he refers to Rush (1981), who had contended that issues such as child sexual abuse and child pornography were not being tackled because men in power did not take them seriously.

Ong (1985) discusses the concept of 'wonderful children', which refers to the tendency to idealise children and concentrate on the positive aspects of bringing them up. The pressures, stresses and pains are paid scant attention and tend to be 'swept under the carpet', thus placing immense additional pressure on women to conform to the idealised norm of a happy, contented mother. In reporting her study of mothers and children at a family centre, B. N. Ong comments:

> [Mothers] are often feeling guilty that they cannot perceive their children in positive ways, and fail to see that this is largely related to factors outside their personal power. Taking women's own experiences as a point of departure, investigating the limitations in their mothering context, can probably instigate more positive change than insisting that all children are wonderful. (p. 105)

The common ideological view of children as 'wonderful' is therefore an additional source of oppression for women.

A further implication of sexism for social work is the casting of women in a caring role. Finch and Groves (1983), present an argument for seeing community care of disabled, mentally disordered or elderly people as primarily care by the family which, in turn, amounts to care by women. As Finch (1983) comments:

> In recent years, feminists have increasingly insisted on making explicit the true meaning of 'community care' as it applies to

elderly or handicapped people, i.e. for community read family, and for family read women, and have rightly been suspicious of attempts to increase such 'community' provision, seeing them as part of the political agenda of getting women out of the labour market and back into the home, to provide unpaid health and welfare services for members of their own family. (p. 6)

A report prepared by the Equal Opportunities Commission (EOC, 1984) showed that elderly people being cared for by men are likely to receive a higher level of state services. It is assumed, apparently, that men will need greater support in undertaking caring tasks.

The EOC also point out that reinforcing the caring role of women is a financially more attractive option than institutional care or care based on comprehensive state services (EOC, 1982). The report goes on to discuss the narrowing of opportunities (for example, for paid employment) experienced by those women who act as carers. The ideological assumption that caring is primarily a female role therefore has profound and far-reaching implications for women in terms of restricted opportunities or life-chances. The discriminatory and oppressive impact of this assumption is therefore of major proportions.

This is a good example of how the familial ideology implicit in social policy manifests itself. Whilst the family as a set of living arrangements has a number of advantages we should not forget:

1. Men derive more benefits from family life than do women. For example, the statistics for suicide attempts show that marital status is very relevant for both men and women – but in opposing ways: the rates for women are *higher* if married but for men the reverse is true as married status indicates a *lower* rate. The clear implication here is that marriage offers more positives and fewer negatives for men than is the case for women.
2. Traditional family roles, and the patriarchal assumptions on which they are based, can have a profoundly alienating effect on women by restricting life-chances, imposing high and often unrealistic expectations in terms of undertaking caring duties and so on.

3. As Laing (1971) and Sennett (1977), amongst others, have argued, the family is a potentially very destructive institution and, given that women act as the lynchpin of the family in the domestic sphere, it is likely that they will suffer the greatest effects and, indeed, be allocated the greater share of the blame. This is particularly significant for social work, operating as it does at the intersection of conflicting forces within the family and the wider social sphere.

Social workers therefore need to adopt a critical stance towards the family, as the traditional social policy eulogy of the family conceals a large number of patriarchal assumptions which fuel the sexism that oppresses women by chaining them to the domestic sphere of caring and nurturing. But social work also needs to look at itself to see sexism as, for example, in the sexual division of labour to be found within social work organisations. Women form the majority of social work clients and social work staff and yet they form a relatively small minority of senior managers (Hallett, 1989b).

Hanmer and Statham (1988) describe the 'double jeopardy' faced by women managers: they have to operate within a predominantly masculine environment and ethos; leadership skills can be seen as 'unfeminine'. Women managers are also expected to prove themselves to justify their place in the 'man's world' of management, and this, of course, adds to the pressures of coping with the demands of the job (Cooper and Davidson, 1982).

The Social Services Inspectorate report on women in Social Services (SSI, 1991) argues that there are many reasons for the under-representation of women in management, not least of which is the stereotyping of women implicit in sexist ideology:

> Women may . . . experience the insidious effects of gender stereotyping, which will not have been such a noticeable feature of their earlier professional careers, when to be a woman was the norm. Examples such as the assumption that a woman is at the meeting to take the minutes, that she will not be able to understand financial matters, or that it is approporiate to may become daily experiences . . . and she may be considered 'humourless' when she fails to laugh at, or draws attention to, sexist comments. (p. 27)

Social work agencies are very clearly not immune from the workings of patriarchy and, indeed, very much reflect them. Occupational segregation in social work is based on a 'sexual division of labour' which parallels the 'dual labour market' (Lash and Urry, 1987; Pond, 1989) with women occupying the majority of lower-status, lower-paid jobs whilst men occupy the majority of more highly paid, higher-status posts.

This has major implications for attempts to develop anti-sexist practice. It needs to be recognised that such endeavours involve 'swimming against the tide' within a male-dominated organisational structure and ethos. And it is this which prompts Dominelli and McLeod (1989) to argue that it is necessary for women to seek support – from like-minded colleagues and managers, trade unions and politicians – if the marginalisation of women is to be countered. Change must therefore take place at an organisational as well as individual level.

There are, of course, very many other implications for social work deriving from sexism but space does not permit a more extensive exposition of the issues. However, I hope the examples given here have raised awareness sufficiently for readers to pursue other issues through further reading and discussion.

The question of how we take forward anti-sexist practice is, of course, a major one and follows on from the discussion here. However, before tackling these issues, we need to be clear about the contribution of feminist theory to this area of social work. In short, it would be unwise to begin to address practice issues without first exploring the theory base – the theoretical formulations of a now well-established tradition of feminist thought. There is now a clear basis for the further development of anti-sexist practice as the emergence of a specifically feminist school of social work has shown (see Langan and Day, 1992). It is therefore important to understand at least the basics of feminist theory.

The feminist response

Williams (1989) presents an account of six different forms of feminism and draws out some of the similarities and differences. This indicates that there is no single consistent and uniform feminism, no simple consensus on the factors underlying male domination and the strategies required to tackle these.

However, this is not to say that there are no common themes or points of agreement. Indeed, they all share a focus on the critique of patriarchy and the need to establish a fairer society in which women are no longer marginalised, alienated and pushed into secondary roles. They also share the belief that 'the personal is political'. This has several levels of meaning:

1. The domestic private sphere also contributes to the wider public and political sphere. For example, housework and childcare are not marginal to the economy but do, in fact, play a key role in maintaining the workings of economic structures and processes.

2. The personal sphere is one dominated by issues of power. Power is not simply a matter of macro-structures relating to large-scale social issues; it also revolves around personal relationships, identity and other such micro-structural aspects of social life.

3. The family is the locus of political struggle. Power, conflict and domination are common aspects of family life. In particular, the power of men over women manifests itself most clearly in the family home in terms of the sexual division of labour, the allocation of leisure time and so on.

4. Gender is *socially constructed* (that is, it hinges on the social significance attached to the differences between men and women) rather than biologically determined. Gender therefore has wider social and political connotations.

5. The oppression of women, and the problems they experience arising from this, are not only 'private troubles' but also 'public issues' (Mills, 1970). Personal problems have their roots in political structures, and political structures are reinforced by a particular form of personal relations (patriarchy).

Feminism therefore seeks to:

● *Politicise the personal*: to draw attention to the political nature and basis of the alienation and oppression of women; and
● *Personalise the political*: to engage women in the collective political struggle for equality of opportunity and equal rights.

The latter is, of course, premised on the heightened awareness achieved by the former. How this struggle should be taken forward is the subject of fierce debate and will no doubt continue to be for some time yet.

The early form of feminism has been labelled 'liberal feminism' and its basic tenets continue to be adhered to by a number of theorists and activists. The emphasis in liberalism is on the individual (Coates, 1990). Individuals are expected to attain differing levels of achievement within social life and the market-place. This is felt to be natural and desirable provided that no individual or group of individuals is unfairly disadvantaged. And this is where liberal feminism comes in – women are felt to be handicapped in competing for jobs, status, power and so on as a result of sexism.

Liberal feminism therefore sees the way forward as a combination of campaigning for equal opportunities, educating people about the problems of discrimination, and generally allowing a fairer basis on which women can compete, on an individual basis, with men. Change is seen as gradual, incremental and based on specific targets for reform.

The liberal feminist focus is, in terms of the PCS model, very much at the *P* level, the personal or individual. And it is this which has been the major source of criticism of this approach. The individualism inherent in liberal feminism is castigated for failing to take account of the wider aspects, particularly the structural nature of power relations and the institutional, rather than personal, sources of discrimination and oppression. It is seen as rather a naïve approach which tinkers with superficial aspects of the problem rather than tackling the social and political roots. This is sometimes expressed in comical (but none the less serious) terms as 'rearranging the deckchairs on the Titanic', that is, maintaining a blinkered view of a structurally-based problem.

However, we should not dismiss liberal feminism altogether. It is more helpful to see it as not going far enough rather than going in the wrong direction. The need, therefore, is not to reject liberal feminism but rather to transcend it. Indeed, liberal feminists could argue that they have achieved significant steps forward in terms of anti-discrimination legislation and a higher level of awareness of gender inequality whilst more structurally-based approaches have achieved little or nothing. This is an important argument for anti-sexist social work and one to which I shall return below.

An alternative perspective is that of radical feminism. In contrast with liberalism, radical feminism focuses on underlying structural and power issues which are seen to hinge on the key concept of *patriarchy*. In radical feminism the dominance of men is seen as a historical constant, a ubiquitous feature of male-dominated relations. Regardless of the type of society – capitalist, pre-capitalist, communist or whatever – men are everywhere to be found in positions of power, including central and local government, economic institutions, the judiciary, the professions and so on.

Mayes (1986) explains Firestone's (1972) views on how patriarchy came to predominate:

> women's reproductive functions have made them dependent on men for much of human history. As women learned to control their fertility and to find alternative forms of support, men learned the techniques to ensure their domination. These were the creation of an ideology which stresses conformity to sharply divided gender roles and an economic system which perpetuates women's financial dependence on men. (p. 80)

This biological dimension of women's oppression is a key part of radical feminism. It emphasises the part played by reproduction and the family structures and ideology that have been constructed around the notion of women primarily as mother figures, thus allowing men to take up the powerful father role (hence the word *patriarchy*).

The strength of the radical perspective is that it recognises the structural dimension of women's oppression and therefore goes much further than the liberal approach that would leave existing power structures relatively untouched. Radical feminism, as the name implies, identifies the need to tackle the problems *at the root*, to redress the power balance between men and women, and this cannot be done by piecemeal reform alone. A more comprehensive programme of social change is called for.

The weakness of this approach is its ahistorical nature. It sees the dominance of men as universal – both across cultures and through history. Thus it has been criticised for placing too much emphasis on the biological underpinnings of sexism and not enough on historical, sociopolitical factors. This leads Walby (1990) to comment as follows:

> The main problems that critics have raised about radical feminism are a tendency to essentialism, to an implicit or explicit biological reductionism, and to a false universalism which cannot understand historical change or take sufficient account of divisions between women based on ethnicity and class. (p. 3)

Marxist-feminism – or socialist feminism as it is often called – shares radical feminism's emphasis on the structural and power base of the oppression of women. However, unlike the radical approach, marxist-feminism focuses not on the biological roots of sexism but rather on its historical and political roots.

Marxist-feminism sees patriarchy as a structure which supports and reinforces capitalism. The family is seen as a microcosm of wider society, in which women represent the proletariat (the exploited class) and men the bourgeoisie (the exploiters) (Engels, 1844). A central part of this is the sexual division of labour, as discussed earlier in this chapter. Men are socialised into the role of workers in the public sphere – *the producers* – whilst women are socialised into the roles of wives and mothers in the private sphere – *the reproducers*. This arrangement is well suited to capitalism as it produces a workforce that is 'serviced' from within the family. In addition, it provides a 'reserve army of labour', a secondary (female) workforce which can be recruited when the economy expands or in exceptional circumstances (for example, men going off to war) and dispensed with when they are no longer required. This is facilitated by the fact that women tend to have less job security than men (McDowell, 1989) and tend to be located lower down the occupational hierarchy.

Marxist-feminism recognises the dual oppressions of capitalism (related to class) and patriarchy (related to gender) and the inter-relationship between the two. As Williams (1989) puts it: 'there can be no socialism without women's liberation, and no women's liberation without socialism' (p. 57). The marxist version of feminism seeks to locate patriarchy within the context of a materialist analysis. That is, patriarchy is not simply a reflection of biological differences between men and women. Rather, it is closely related to the production of material life, that is, the economic base.

This link with the economy is precisely one of the strong points of marxist-feminism. It succeeds in relating the power of men over women to the capitalist class over the working class.

This emphasis on class is also perhaps the main weakness of marxist-feminism, however. The main focus of explanation is the economic base and the class divisions on which it rests. This leads to a relative weakness in terms of explaining the dominance of men over women in non-capitalist societies, for example, agrarian societies.

There are, of course, other forms of feminism that have something to offer to an understanding of women's oppression. But what is clear is that there is no single right answer, no definitive feminism. The debates and struggles continue and, from a social work point of view, the positive thing to note is that the issues are now more firmly established on the professional agenda than ever before.

The approaches to feminism are not static and fixed. For example, Brenner and Ramas (1990), building on the work of Barrett (1980), seek to incorporate elements of radical feminism, within a marxist-feminist framework. And what is perhaps most significant is that there is now a growing body of literature on feminism and social work (for example, Hanmer and Statham, 1988; Dominelli and McLeod, 1989; Van den Bergh and Cooper, 1986; Dominelli, 1991; Langan and Day, 1992).

Sexism and men

There are two aspects to the question of men and sexism: first, what impact does sexism have on men? And second, what part can men play in undermining, reducing or eliminating sexism?

Whilst the actions and attitudes of men are often a significant source of pressure and difficulty for women as a result of the potent and far-reaching influence of sexist ideology, it cannot be said that sexism is unproblematic for men. Men clearly do benefit from the power and privilege invested in them by patriarchy. However, it must also be recognised – and this is a very important potential source of change – that men also suffer as a result of sexism (although clearly not to the same extent or depth as women). Dominelli and McLeod (1989) raise a number of issues in relation to the negative impact of sexism on men:

● the capacity for emotional engagement is restricted and distorted by the emphasis on stereotypical masculine traits (p. 5);
● Cartledge and Ryan (1983) argue that men experience emotional deprivation as a result of sexism (p. 11);
● Festau (1975) is used as an example of how men are beginning to question 'the price of being thought superior' (p. 70);
● 'relationships, centred on domination and subordination are not only injurious to women's needs but also stultifying for the men concerned (Tolson, 1977)' (p. 95);
● consequently the dissolution of sexism will benefit men's welfare in the longer term (p. 6).

Hearn (1987), Hudson (1989) and Nelson (1990) use the dehumanisation inherent in sexism as the basis of an argument for men adopting a pro-feminist stance in opposing sexism. As Nelson puts it, the aim is not to 'let men off the hook'. It is, rather, to recognise that anti-sexism is a battle to be fought not only by women but also by men, partly for their own emotional emancipation and partly for humanitarian reasons as a step towards the dissolution of oppressive structures and practices. It would be naïve indeed to assume that men would readily give up the advantages of patriarchy but this should not deter us from seeing the benefits of anti-sexism for both women and men.

Men therefore have a part to play in furthering the cause of anti-sexism. A major aspect of this is the need to become sensitive to the part men play in reproducing sexist structures and cultural patterns in and by their actions and attitudes. In short, both men and women need to be aware of how their actions (the P level) can avoid pushing them into the trap of reinforcing and reproducing the sexism inherent in the C and S levels – and, indeed, can even go so far as to challenge those patterns and structures.

Towards anti-sexist practice

Although there is a growing body of literature on anti-sexist theory and policy, this is unlikely to have an impact unless it is put into practice. It is therefore necessary to focus on some of the ways in which anti-sexist practice can be made a reality.

Of course, there can be no single 'formula' approach to putting anti-sexist theory into practice, but identifying some broad principles may help us to move in the right direction.

1. The aim of social work intervention is empowerment, *not* adjustment. The social work task should not be to help women to adjust to their 'rightful' place in the family but rather to assist them in gaining the power to overcome or challenge the oppression they experience. The personal is, after all, political.

2. An important, indeed major, part of this is the need to avoid stereotypical assumptions. We should not assume, for example, that the male is the head of the household and the primary decision-maker in a two-parent family. If we are not careful, assessing family dynamics can be reduced to jumping to sexist conclusions.

3. Similarly, in childcare cases, in addition to focusing on the child(ren), work should be directed towards *parents* rather than simply mothers. If not, we run the risk of

'mother-blaming' and reinforcing the notion that women carry the primary responsibility for the family.

4. The sexist implications of the notion of 'community care' need to be addressed. This entails resisting the pressure to push women into caring roles. Sexist ideology leads us to believe that it is 'natural' for women to be carers and this can, unless we guard against it, allow us to ignore or marginalise the intense pressures which can be inherent in the caring role.

5. Familial ideology reinforces sexism by emphasising the positives of family life and playing down the negatives. Social workers are well aware of the destructive capabilities of families but may none the less be seduced by familial ideology into uncritically promoting the value of the family. Social work practice needs to be based on a balanced view of the value of the family which recognises both its strengths and its weaknesses.

6. Clients too are strongly influenced by familial ideology in particular and sexist ideology in general. Whilst the primary task of social work is not the dissolution of sexism, consciousness-raising is often necessary to help service users understand how sexism may be contributing to their problems or acting as a barrier to the solution of their problems. This parallels the radical social work principle of helping people recognise the political basis of many of the problems commonly experienced (poverty, bad housing, alienation and so on).

7. It has been argued that social workers often portray women in unduly negative terms as 'helpless' or 'not coping' (Rojek *et al.*, 1989, p. 93) in order to gain additional resources for them. This tactic has the effect of producing enforced dependency and is therefore one to be avoided.

8. Women are 'invisible' within a male-dominated society in so far as their achievements and contributions are rarely given due credit. Social workers need to avoid this trap and appropriately value women, their thoughts, feelings and work. At a micro level, social work can contribute to enhanced self-esteem for women clients (and staff) and at

a macro level play at least a small part in the breaking down of the sexist devaluation of women.

9. Sexual harassment is also an important issue: 'Unwelcome sexual comments, looks, actions, suggestions or physical contact can cause great distress to women and damage confidence, job performance and promotion prospects' (SSI, 1991, p. 53). This can be applied both to female colleagues and to clients. Much sexual harassment is unintentional, based on an insensitivity to women's needs and feelings but is none the less oppressive. Anti-sexist social work must challenge intentional forms of harassment and develop a sensitivity to unintentional forms.

10. Anti-sexist practice involves challenging dominant discriminatory attitudes, values, practices and structures. It entails 'problematising', that is, taking everyday, apparently unproblematic matters and showing just how problematic they are, highlighting just how discriminatory and oppressive they really are. This includes Berger's (1966) notion of 'debunking', or Mills' (1970) 'sociological imagination'. In short, it amounts to questioning assumptions about men and women in society and involves adopting a *critical* approach.

There are many more points and examples which could be given to build on these basics (see, for example, the 'Code of Practice for Non-sexist Woman-centred Social Work', in Hanmer and Statham (1988) pp. 139–43).

4

Ethnicity and Racism

Britain, it is often said, is a multi-cultural society. That is, it is composed of a variety of ethnic groups each with different characteristics and patterns. How important this is for social work forms the major analytical focus of this chapter. Storkey (1991) defines ethnicity as:

> all the characteristics which go to make up cultural identity; origins, physical appearance, language, family structure, religious beliefs, politics, food, art, music, literature, attitudes towards the body, gender roles, clothing, education. (pp. 109–10)

The term is particularly significant when used to describe minority groups within a society; that is, ethnic minorities. As Storkey suggests, it is often forgotten that all people are 'ethnic', that is, belong to a cultural group, and so it is both inaccurate and misleading to refer to members of ethnic minorities as 'ethnics' or 'ethnic people'. This implies that to be a member of the ethnic majority is 'normal' and so members of ethnic minorities are by definition deviant. This, as we shall see below, is a form of racism.

But ethnicity is only one part of the situation; it is by no means the whole story. Ethnicity implies *difference* whereas the dominant notion social workers encounter is that of *deficit*. Members of ethnic minorities are often perceived as being inferior and are thus subject to discrimination. Ethnic minority groups are presented ideologically, as biologically different from and, by implication, inferior to, the ethnic majority. In this way, ethnic difference (characterised by solidarity, shared values and positively valued cultural identity) is constructed as racial inferiority (characterised by

58

exclusion, marginalisation and oppression). It is therefore important to see ethnicity and race in conjunction, as the cultural differences of ethnicity are used as a political weapon to reinforce the power of the dominant majority in so far as these differences are seen as deviations from the ethnocentric norm.

Failure to recognise this covert shift from ethnicity to race serves to mask racism and its subtle influences. Rex (1986) comments: 'The attempt to assimilate racial to ethnic problems, therefore, often led to the interpretation of racial problems not as forms of conflict but as benign phenomena of difference' (p.19). In short, Britain, the USA and other Western countries are indeed multi-cultural but to focus exclusively on cultural or ethnic patterns without taking account of 'race' is indeed a naïve mistake. Race is not a biological category, it is a process – a social and political process whereby ethnic differences are translated into pseudo-biological racial deficits. In this way the seeds of racism are sown. Discrimination against black and ethnic minority peoples is legitimated on the basis of assumed racial inferiority. This is a point to which I shall return below.

Social workers dealing with a wide range of ethnic communities therefore need to be aware of ethnic differences (ethnically sensitive social work) and the commonalities across minority groups, that is oppression, discrimination and relative powerlessness (anti-racist social work). This chapter seeks to establish a clearer understanding of the racial dimension of social work and take steps toward the development of an anti-racist social work practice base. The first step towards this must be a clarification of the central concept of racism.

What is racism?

Lorde (1984) defines racism as the: 'belief in the inherent superiority of one race over all others and thereby the right to dominance, manifest and implied' (quoted in Dominelli, 1989b, p. 392).

This gets us off to a good start in terms of understanding what racism is but, in itself, is not enough to give the clarification we need. A fuller definition is offered by Chakrabarti (1990):

> Racism is, first a set of beliefs or a way of thinking within which groups identified on the basis of real or imagined biological characteristics (skin colour, for example) are thought necessarily to possess other characteristics that are viewed in a negative light . . . It is rooted in the belief that certain groups, identified as 'races', 'ethnic minorities' or by some more abusive label, share characteristics such as attitudes or abilities and a propensity to certain behaviour. The assumption is made that every person, whether man, woman or child, classified as belonging to such a group, is possessed of all these characteristics. (p. 15)

This definition includes a number of key elements:

1. Beliefs and values are a basic part of racism; that is, racism is an *ideology*.
2. It relates to 'real or imagined biological characteristics'. Racism is therefore socially constructed rather than biologically given (Pilkington, 1984, p. 18).
3. Racism is a negative term: it has strong negative connotations and is used as a form of abuse (and, by extension, discrimination and oppression).
4. Stereotypical assumptions are used to sustain this negativity and thus to maintain the dominance, power and privilege of the white majority.

A simpler and better-known definition is that of Katz (1978): 'prejudice plus power'. This is useful in so far as it points out that racism is more than just a matter of personal prejudice but is indeed a much wider issue. However, this definition and the approach of Katz in general have been discredited, as we shall see in my discussion below of 'race awareness training'.

Racism can be seen to operate at all three levels of the PCS model: *P* – personal prejudice is an important part of the complex matrix of racism. Many people hold explicitly racist views and may even be members of racialist organisations such as the National Front. However, personal prejudice also manifests itself much more subtly and we are not likely to be aware of it unless and until we are confronted. *C* – racist jokes, cultural stereotypes and assumptions of white superiority are all to be found at the *C* level. Popular notions of black and white are imbued with racism as cultural or ethnic differences are reframed as examples of cultural deficit. Patterns, values, behaviour or any kind of norm which differs from that of the white majority is construed as being inferior. *S* – race is an important aspect of social stratification and the differential allocation of power to individuals and groups in society. Racism is built in to the structure of society and its dominant institutions. The discrimination and oppression experienced by people from ethnic minorities is not simply individual prejudice but rather a reflection of discriminatory structures and institutional practices.

There are a number of implications which arise from this. First, we must be aware of the mistake so often made in the past – that is to focus too much attention on the individual level and see prejudice as the basis or 'cause' of racism. It takes one part of the whole, separates it from the wider context in which it is embedded and presents it as the 'whole story'. As Husband (1991) puts it:

> The importance of this analysis is that it reduces racism to human nature and individual fallibility, thus leaving the world of the state, the world of politics and major structural aspects of contemporary life out of focus. (p. 50)

Similarly, Sivanandan (1991) points out the weakness inherent in the Scarman Report of 1982 which also laid too great a stress on the *P* level. He puts this point across quite strongly in the following passage:

> Basically, Scarman said there is no institutional racism but there is racial prejudice. He took away the objective facts of institutional racism and made them subjective. So that what we had to tackle was not the system, not the power, not the police on the streets, not the immigration officers who examined my sister to see if she was a virgin. What we had to change was the immigration officer's mind, so that he would not dislike my sister. That is nonsense. (p. 42)

The PCS analysis also alerts us to the fact that racism is not necessarily intentional. In reflecting dominant cultural values or carrying out routine institutional practices, we may actually be perpetrating acts of racism unwittingly. For example, working on the premise that Asian families 'look after their own' may prevent Asian clients from receiving the service they require. Although this may not be racist in *intention*, it is none the less racist in *effect* or *outcome* and is likely to be experienced as oppressive.

In this respect, and indeed many others, racism can be seen to parallel sexism. For example, Shah (1989) argues that: 'Racism and sexism work in similar ways by discriminating against people and by reinforcing stereotyping' (p. 179). There are indeed important parallels in the processes which underpin both sexism and racism. Thus in seeking to understand racism, looking to our knowledge of sexism can help us move forward. However, we must none the less avoid the mistake of allowing the similarities to distract us from the significant differences (for example, the role of sexuality in sexism or the residue of imperialism in racism).

Brah and Deem (1986) capture the point succinctly as follows: 'Sexism and racism as social divisions have a number of features in common although they are certainly not comparable in every way' (pp. 66–7). Dominelli (1988), referring to the work of Bromley and Longino (1972), also lays stress on appreciating the three levels of racism – individual, cultural and institutional. From this she moves on to discuss the 'new racism' (Barker, 1981). This refers to the movement away from the traditional racist emphasis on biology to a 'new racism' which plays down the significance of biological differences but retains a discriminatory focus by inserting cultural difference in their place. As with the 'old racism', difference is then equated with deficit. Racist ideology readily leads to the assumption that any culture which is different from the dominant white culture is necessarily an inferior culture.

Husband (1991) points out that the ability of 'new racists' to reject 'the vulgar biological theory of Darwinian scientific racism' (p. 63) actually strengthens their ability to promote their culturally-based racism. By distancing themselves from the easily discredited biologism, proponents of the 'new racism' can more easily continue to maintain their racist views.

Both old and new racism serve to 'pathologise' black individuals and families, to present them as inferior to, and therefore less worthy than, their white counterparts. This tendency is also visible in social work and therefore has major implications for practice. As Ahmed (1991) puts it:

> Negative images of black family life have crept into social work and social policy analysis. The Afro-Caribbean family is often seen as a tangle of pathology, virtually non-existent as a unit or rapidly falling apart, with mothers being seen as too strong and committed to wage-earning. On the other hand, the Asian family is seen as problematic because the mother's position is considered weak and uninfluential. (p. 174) (See also Ahmed *et al.*, 1986; and Ahmed, 1987.)

Such negative stereotypes serve to reinforce the process of pathologising individuals, families and cultures that 'deviate' from the dominant white norm. This is one example among many of the implications of racism for social work policy, theory and practice. It is a discussion of these issues which forms the basis of the next section.

The implications for social work

One very clear implication to be drawn from the literature on racism and social work is that traditional social work has seriously neglected the racial dimension of the social problems it seeks to tackle and the impact of racism on ethnic minority communities.

It even goes beyond this to the point where social work practice is itself racist, whether by acts of omission or commission, whether deliberate or unwitting. Dominelli (1989b) expresses it in this way:

> The subtle dynamics of personal, institutional and cultural racism permeate the routine minutiae of social work policy and practice and these, combined with the strategies white social workers

utilise to avoid confronting racism in their work, mean that black people's needs receive short shrift. (p. 391)

This is not to say that social workers are 'racists' who deliberately try to short-change their black clients. The actions of social workers need to be seen in their wider cultural and structural context. Rooney (1980) captures this point well in the following passage:

> And it's hard to accept that in the work we do daily, with its humanitarian and Christian ethics, we may be a part of a process of institutionalised racism. But hard though that may be, it is too easy to dissociate ourselves in clear conscience from the part that we play in the subtle, sophisticated strategies of racial discrimination, which despite apparent well-meaning and good intent at every level, still leaves blacks worse off by the time the process works its way through. (p. 51)

At one level it is indeed hard to believe that 'nice people' such as social workers could contribute so strongly to discrimination and oppression. However, at another level, they are part of a wider framework that reflects power and privilege differences and which hinges on social divisions. This therefore brings us back to the point emphasised earlier, namely, if you are not part of the solution you must be part of the problem.

Racism operates via acts of omission as well as commission and so the excuse that we were not aware of 'the problem' is not a valid one. When we become aware of the racism inherent in the culture and institutions of social work (the *C* and *S* levels) our own actions (the *P* level) will either reflect, reinforce and consolidate such racism or may go at least some small way towards challenging and undermining it. There can be no neutral territory.

One way in which racism manifests itself in social work is in the over-representation of black people in 'control' situations and under-representation in 'care' situations. The criminal and juvenile justice fields provide many instances of racist assumptions serving to prejudice black defendants' treatment in the courts. For example, Whitehouse (1986) undertook a study of social inquiry reports prepared in respect of black clients. He cites many examples of reports which are premised on racist assumptions and therefore increase the chances of a harsher sentence being imposed.

He describes the situation whereby stereotypical assumptions may trigger off a process which can have very negative consequences for the client:

> Thus if the social worker has stereotypical expectations and attitudes he or she will tend to select information to confirm them. If the persons under assessment perceive themselves to be the object of categorical or stereotypical assessment, they will tend to withdraw from the interaction, to give as little information and collaboration as possible. This may well be interpreted by the more powerful in the interaction as uncooperative behaviour or having 'something to hide'. (p. 117)

Hutchinson-Reis (1989) gives similar examples and adds that, whilst social work is perhaps no more racist than other state institutions, the 'progressive facade' of social work enables it to obscure or conceal the underlying racism (p. 171). The power of the social worker or probation officer in court is considerable, given the high percentage of social inquiry report recommendations accepted by the courts. Where this power is premised on racist assumptions, the disservice to the black clients is likely to be of major proportions.

Ahmad (1990) makes similar points concerning mental health social work in relation to black people. She points to the growing literature on the subject and comments that:

> It is well acknowledged that Mental Health services are involved in social control and as such Mental Health professionals have power to enforce controlling functions, including the law. The correlation between over-representation of Black people in Mental Health services and exposure to social control is not hard to identify. (p. 31)

There are (at least) two key aspects to this, first misdiagnosis through a lack of of cultural understanding or even overt racism (Cope, 1989, p. 351), and second, the fact that: 'Many black people become mentally ill as a result of the systematic erosion of their capacity to deal with multiple oppressions'

(Pennie Pennie, chair of ABSWAP, quoted in Whyte, 1989, p. 24).

In relation to the first point, Francis (1991a) comments on the need for the Afro-Caribbean Mental Health Association to provide a legal advice and representation service, such are the numbers of black people who feel they have been wrongfully detained in hospital under the Mental Health Act, 1983. Many studies refer to the over-representation of black and ethnic minority people in terms of the diagnosis of schizophrenia (Ineichen, 1989). A frequently cited explanation of this is the tendency to 'over-diagnose' brought about by a lack of understanding of the patient's culture and the ways in which distress and emotion are handled. As Whyte (1989) puts it: 'How can a white, middle-class male psychiatrist know how a young Afro-Caribbean man expresses grief or how an Asian woman deals with depression' (p. 23). This has become the basis of what is known as 'transcultural psychiatry' (Rack, 1982) and it is an important step towards ethnically sensitive practice – a practice which seeks to avoid the pitfalls of a distorted diagnosis based on an inadequate appreciation of cultural patterns, values and norms. This is a *necessary* condition for anti-racism but, as we shall see below in the discussion of multi-culturalism, it is not a *sufficient* condition.

Inappropriate use of powers under the Mental Health Act 1983 is an easy trap for social workers to fall into if they are not sufficiently aware of the racial dimension of psychiatry, their own potential for racism and that of other professionals within the mental health field.

In relation to the second point, the impact of racism on mental health, Pennie's comments draw a clear causal link between racism and mental disorder. Burke (1986), however, takes a more cautious view. He argues, in relation to second and third generation West Indians in Britain that: 'High rates of unemployment . . . together with inadequate housing and education, will have the effect of identifying a socially deprived group that is likely to be over-admitted to mental hospital facilities' (p. 179). Whether these social circumstances lead to more psychiatric admissions by 'causing' mental illness or by triggering racial prejudice within the psychiatric system remains an open question. This is indeed a complex area (see

Burke, 1984, for further discussion of this debate), but one thing which is clear is that racism plays an important part in the over-representation of black people within the statutory mental health field.

Similar arguments apply to the over-representation of black children in care. Heptinstall (1986) refers to estimates of as many as 60 per cent of children in care in some areas being from ethnic minority groups. Roys (1988) gives more precise figures but acknowledges that:

> The reasons for this disturbing state of affairs are complex, but it can be argued that black consumers may enter a downward spiral, resulting in statutory action which might have been avoided were extensive and effective services available at an earlier stage. (p. 210)

He contends that this is due to two factors. On the one hand, black people are reluctant to become involved with white institutions except as a last resort, and on the other, white social workers may be reluctant to engage with black families, whether due to overt racism, or as a consequence of 'liberal overcompensation' (p. 211) as, for example, in the Jasmine Beckford case in which child protection issues were overlooked in an attempt to 'identify' with the black family.

These examples of the over-representation of black people in 'control' situations are paralleled by an equivalent under-representation in 'caring' or supportive services. Numerous sources refer to the relative neglect of black communities in terms of the provision of supportive social services (Roys, 1988; Duncan, 1986; Rooney, 1987; Dominelli, 1989b; and Ahmad, 1990).

Social work has long been recognised as a mixture of care and control and, to a large extent, these two elements represent two sides of the same coin. However, the situation in relation to black and ethnic minority clients is that there is a distinct imbalance. The control element is very much to the fore whilst the caring element features far less than is the case with white clients. Dominelli (1988) refers to this as 'an emphasis on social control at the expense of caring' (pp. 28–9). She then goes on to add that 'Racism exacerbates and extends social control in social work' (p. 29).

What this demonstrates is that racism not only acts as a barrier to good practice but actually 'uses' social work as a vehicle for further discrimination and oppression. As Mercer (1984) puts it: 'you don't have to take an anti-social work stance to be aware of how some of the functions of social work reproduce and reinforce institutional racism' (p. 24, quoted in Roys, 1988, p. 209).

This relates to the point made in Chapter 1 – that good practice must be anti-discriminatory practice; a social work which is unaware of its discriminatory potential is a dangerous social work.

These issues are particularly pertinent to the process of assessment – gauging the nature and extent of the problems and the resources available or needed. There are two main sets of issues involved. First, there is the cultural dimension. There is a danger that assessment will be based on dominant white norms without adequate attention being paid to cultural differences. Failure to take such differences into account will not only distort, and thereby invalidate, the basis of the assessment but will also serve to alienate clients by devaluing their culture.

But this means more than distinguishing between white culture and 'black culture' for there is no one single black culture. Black cultures are many and varied and to ignore this is to operate at a stereotypical level, to oversimplify a complex picture. Ethnically sensitive social work involves developing at least a basic understanding of local ethnic minority communities and cultures. Social work assessment needs to be based on understanding and analysis rather than ignorance and assumptions.

Henley (1986) discusses Asian communities in Britain and comments that:

> Each group tends to see itself as separate and distinct from the others, and the different groups originally settled separately, drawn to different employment offers and prospects. Lumping people together and seeing them as a single, culturally homogeneous group is therefore very misleading. It is about as useful as lumping people together as Europeans. A Sikh from Punjab and a Muslim from Bangladesh are likely to have as much and as

little in common as a Catholic from Spain and a Protestant from Sweden. (p. 37)

And, of course, the cultural pluralism is further extended by the fact that a significant and growing proportion of black people (estimated to be 40 per cent – Jacobs, 1988) were born in Britain and have therefore been brought up under the influence of the culture of their parents and the dominant white culture as transmitted by the media, the education system and so on.

Black communities are therefore different, both from each other and from the white majority – this is the dimension of *ethnicity*. What social work assessment also needs to take into account is what black communities have in common – their experience of *racism*. As Ahmed (1987) puts it:

> I am not against better cultural understanding but I am against an *over-reliance* on cultural explanations which distract attention both from significant emotional factors as well as structural factors such as class and race. This important point is that for Black clients, the centrality of racism, needs to be more explicitly acknowledged in the assessment process and cultural explanations need to be considered in the context of racism. (p. 6)

It is perhaps easier and less uncomfortable for us to take on board cultural diversity without going a step further and acknowledging racism and the need to challenge it (Ely and Denney, 1987). There are times when we can indulge in seeing the rich variety of cultural patterns as a contribution to social life, an 'entertainment' to make white lives more interesting, but without also recognising the disadvantages and discrimination ethnic minority communities experience (Cheetham, 1981, p. 6).

Fernando (1989) warns of the dangers of reducing race to culture and thereby side-stepping the difficult and painful task of challenging racism. He comments:

> An emphasis on culture, however well-intentioned, may lead to a racist approach in practice . . . the promotion of cultural sensitivity without challenging racism may result in the reinforcement of racism by masking it and thereby inducing complacency. (p. 167)

Cultural awareness promotes ethnically sensitive practice and thus helps to avoid the problems of devaluing minority cultures or seeing them as inferior to white culture, and thereby alienating the people who share those cultures. This is a valuable step forward but, as Fernando warns, it is also necessary to take the further step of recognising elements of racism in ourselves, our practice and our agencies. It is only then that we can move towards *anti-racist* practice.

One aspect of the relationship between racism and social work that is often not appreciated is that the foundations of anti-racist social work are actually enshrined in legislation:

> The Race Relations Act 1976 makes discrimination on racial grounds unlawful, and places a statutory duty on local authorities to make appropriate arrangements to ensure that their functions are carried out with due regard for the need to eliminate unlawful discrimination and to promote equality of opportunity and good relations. (Woolfe and Malahleka, 1990, p. 5)

Of course, it would be naïve to assume that such a broad legislative statement could ensure a firm foundation for anti-racist practice. A tighter and much more specific set of policy guidelines and regulations would be necessary to provide such a baseline for anti-discriminatory policies which can readily be translated into practice.

Ahmad (1990) makes a similar point when she comments that:

> No legislation alone can make social workers anti-racist. Much depends on how they interpret the laws or even abuse them to reinforce racism. Much also depends on how legislations are used as a tool to tackle racism in social work. (p. 5)

Racism is a powerful force in society. It subjects one portion of society – black and ethnic minority groups – to oppression, degradation and discrimination on the grounds that they are deemed to be inferior, by virtue of biology and/or culture, to the white majority.

When we consider this carefully it becomes clear that this situation has major implications for social work in terms of policies, theory base, practice, training, recruitment and management. Space does not permit a detailed analysis of these issues but I shall return later in this chapter to focus specifically on some of the practice implications.

Having drawn, albeit rather sketchily, some of the links between racism and social work, let us now consider some of the factors leading to the development of the modern approach to anti-racism.

The anti-racist response

Although there have been black communities in Britain for centuries, it was in the late 1940s and early 1950s that race relations issues began to take on increasing significance as a result of specific historical developments at that time.

In the years following the end of the Second World War there were labour shortages which, it was felt, would hold back the promised new age of prosperity and post-war reconstruction. It was therefore deemed necessary to seek out new sources of labour to expand the workforce and thus sustain economic development The New Commonwealth countries were seen as a rich seam of potential workers and so these areas were targeted for an intensive advertising and promotional campaign to persuade possible recruits to emigrate to Britain. This campaign was successful and led to a rise in Britain's black population (although not as great as contemporary media reports suggested; see Miles and Solomos, 1987).

However, what this campaign did not emphasise was that the jobs available were the lowest paid and the least popular. It was also not made clear that no additional health or educational facilities would be provided. In particular, the failure to consider housing need exacerbated the existing housing shortage, which meant that the vast majority of the invited immigrants lived in very poor quality conditions in seriously overcrowded accommodation.

The link between race and class became strongly established as black people very quickly became over-represented at the lower levels of Britain's socioeconomic class system. (The relationship between class and race is an important one, and one to which I shall return later.) It was not long before black people were seen not as the victims of poverty, inadequate housing and so on but as a significant part of the *cause* of such problems.

An attitude of racial superiority among the white 'hosts' was instrumental in translating the structurally-based problems experienced by black people into matters of personal failing, weakness or inadequacy – poverty caused by 'not working hard enough', poor housing by having 'lower standards'. The next step was to blame black people for the problems experienced by white people: 'they take our jobs', and 'they cause trouble'. This was the emergence of racism on a much wider scale than ever before. The focus was not on the problems of black people brought about by the government's poorly-thought-out migrant labour policy but rather on black people *as a problem*. The pattern persists to this day: the problem of racism is conveniently reframed as the problem of race.

An early response to this situation was the development of what became known as the *assimilationist* approach. The proposed solution was that black people should integrate as far as possible into mainstream white society so that they did not attract hostility by being 'too different'. In short, the answer to white hostility was seen as black people becoming 'white' in all but skin colour Once again we see an implicit notion of racial superiority – adopting white norms is seen as advantageous to black people. The loss of ethnicity and cultural 'belongingness' is not considered important and the development of a positive black identity is obstructed. According to this model, the best that a black person can become is 'almost white'.

A significant aspect of this approach is the attempt to seek to minimise differences between black and white. The assimilationist approach is therefore characterised as 'colour-blind'. In social work this amounts to ignoring the different needs of ethnic minority groups (brought about in no small part by the impact of racism) (Connelly, 1988). Roys (1988) describes this approach in the following terms:

> Members of the black communities who require services would simply be allocated to existing categories of need. The possibility

of significant differences between black and white consumers within these categories which may indicate a need for modification or substantial change to the services provided is not recognized, nor is consideration given to the possibility that entirely new services might be necessary. (p. 213)

A very different but similarly problematic approach that follows a different logic is that of *multi-culturalism*. The emphasis here is not on minimising differences between black and white but rather on *cultural diversity*. The differences between white 'mainstream' culture and the various black cultures are given due regard, in theory at least, and such differences can actually be celebrated as enriching the cultural life of all. Ethnicity is positively valued and diversity is presented as a potential benefit rather than a problem.

Up to a point, this is a significant improvement on the assimilationist position, as it does avoid the problems of sweeping ethnic differences under the carpet. However, it does not go far enough and, albeit unintentionally, can actually allow racism to persist but in a more respectable form. As Ahmed (1991) comments:

> This perspective regards other cultures as valuable and interesting but ignores the fundamental fact that cultures are ranked in order of merit in British society and black cultures are ranked very low indeed . . . This model aims to promote better understanding but demonstrates little regard for racial justice. It ignores the power relations between black and white people in history and in the present. (p. 168) (See also Williams, 1989, pp. 92–5; and Sivanandan, 1991)

An approach that did not ignore power was that of race awareness training or 'RAT' as it became known. RAT was based on Katz's (1978) definition of racism as 'prejudice plus power'. However, the sort of power to which it referred was that of individuals by virtue of their job or status (Sivanandan, 1991, p. 43) rather than social or political power on a wider structural basis A further problem with this approach was that its attempts to tackle racial prejudice were based on an aggressive, confrontational approach and, as Gurnah (1984) points out, this was, in fact, counterproductive in so far as it resulted in helping 'white liberals to cope better with their guilt without making any real changes in their behaviour' (Ferns, 1987, p. 21). Or, as Husband (1986) puts it: 'Race awareness training can produce a socially competent non-racist performance; it does not produce an anti-racist practice' (p. 11).

These various approaches to 'race relations' have all failed to address the central feature of the problem, namely *racism*, premised on:

1. The hostility of white people to black;
2. The assumed superiority which legitimates this; and
3. The unequal distribution of power, privilege, resources and life-chances which such hostility sustains.

Roys (1988) once again makes apt comment:

> The difficulties faced by the black population are the result not only of migration and differences in culture and language but also of living in a society which is hostile to black people, denies them equal life chances and can expose them to enormous material and psychological pressure. The clients of social services present with not only linguistic and cultural complexities but also with the profound effects of racism. (p. 221)

Modern anti-racism dismisses the oppression and 'cultural imperialism' of assimilationism and transcends the cultural pluralism of multiculturalism. It recognises the structural basis of racism and how this underpins the cultural and personal dimensions of racial discrimination (as in the PCS model outlined in Chapter 2).

How anti-racism can be made a reality in social work practice will be discussed below, but we must first clarify, to a certain extent at least, the relationships between race and class on the one hand and race and gender on the other.

Race, class and gender

The presence of black communities in Britain is not only an issue of race but also of class. The primary reason for the initial migration of black people was the capitalist economy's need to boost its workforce – to extend the working class. Also, as was noted above, the jobs that were available to be filled were low-paid and of low status and thus at the bottom of the class hierarchy. There are close links between race and class. Indeed, racism can be seen as an ideology which divides the working class by setting worker against worker and thereby contributes to the continuance of capitalism by discouraging working-class solidarity (Hall, 1980). However, it is a mistake to see the social division of race as a sub-category of class. Class and race articulate together; that is, they are interrelated. Race remains, however, 'relatively autonomous' from class relations: 'neither totally dependent upon them nor totally abstracted from them' (Williams, 1989, p. 101).

Hall (1980) argues that there are complex interactions of class and racial factors and there is a need to understand these in historically specific terms. That is, the relationship between race and class is not fixed once and for all – it is constantly changing and developing. It is a dynamic relationship which is part of – and has an impact on – other oppressive structures and social forces. He argues that racism:

> has an effect on other ideological formations within the same society, and its development promotes a transformation of the whole ideological field in which it becomes operative. It can harness other ideological discourses to itself – for example, it articulates securely with the us/them structure of corporate class consciousness. (p. 342)

Similarly, Miles (1989) argues that 'contextualising the impact of racism within class relations' has the effect of demonstrating the linkages with other forms of oppression or 'exclusion' (p. 134). In short, racism should not be seen in a vacuum, separate from class and economic factors but neither should it be seen as a by-product or subcategory of the social division of class.

This parallels the debate in Chapter 3 about the relationship between capitalism and patriarchy. But what we now need to consider is the third aspect of the class/race/gender triangle – the relationship between race and gender.

Feminism, in its earlier formulations at least, has been characterised by an emphasis on the common oppression of women, the shared experience of 'sisterhood'. However, the appropriateness of such an emphasis has increasingly been called into question. It is argued that the tendency to focus almost exclusively on the commonalities of women's experience leads to a disregard for significant differences between women, particularly in terms of race.

This has been a significant omission. Parmar (1982), referring to the work of Joseph (1981), comments on a tendency for white feminists to ignore racism and to see the struggles of black women simply as elements of the wider feminist campaign: 'They have thus failed to accommodate the specificity of black women's experiences of racism which have been structured by *racially constructed gender roles*' (p. 237).

In the same volume, Hazel Carby adopts a similar line of argument in proposing that white feminists must adopt an anti-racist stance in order to allow a feminism which is not racially oppressive to develop. She captures the point very clearly in this passage:

> it is very important that white women in the women's movement examine the ways in which racism excludes many black women and prevents them from unconditionally aligning themselves with white women. Instead of taking black women as the objects of their research, white feminist researchers should try to uncover the gender-specific mechanisms of racism amongst white women. This more than any other factor disrupts the recognition of common interests of sisterhood. (1982, p. 232)

Ramazanoglu (1989) extends this argument to include other divisions between women, for example sexual orientation, and this reinforces the critique of an over-simplified analysis of women's experience of oppression. Ramazanoglu also points to the class dimension inherent in the attack on white feminism when she underlines the highly educated middle class ethos of the movement (p. 129), which no doubt further fuelled the anger of the critics.

The theme of anti-sexism failing to take on board issues of anti-racism has been a recurring one. It features in the work of hooks (1982, 1986); Amos *et al.* (1984); Foster-Carter (1987); Bhavnani and Coulson (1986); and Williams (1987), as well as the authors already mentioned. In sum, 'a feminism which ignores racial divisions is open to serious criticism' (Allen, 1987, p. 174). However, there is clearly a growing awareness of the need for feminism to incorporate an anti-racist perspective and the implications of this are in the process of being worked out – see, for example, Dominelli and McLeod, 1989; and Langan and Day, 1992).

It has been recognised that it is not simply a matter of 'tagging on' racism to sexism, as the complex interactions of the two need to be explored and clarified. For, as Bryan *et al.*, (1985) point out, racism can actually change the nature of how sexism is experienced: 'Our relationship with men – both Black and white – have meant that in addition to racism, Black women have had to confront a form of sexism and sexual abuse which is unique to us' (p. 212, quoted in Allen, 1987, p. 173).

The dynamic interplay of class, race and gender is indeed complex and multi-faceted. And, indeed, it will continue to be so as this is an ongoing dynamic, historically variable and far beyond a simple once-and-for-all solution. Although very complex, this is an area where social workers need to have at least a basic grasp of the fundamental issues in order to construct an adequate theoretical basis for anti-discrimina-tory practice.

Towards anti-racist practice

Distilling the principles of anti-racist social work is by no means an easy task, especially as this is a rapidly changing area and one prone to considerable political conflict and widely differing sets of values. Nonetheless, the remainder of this chapter is an attempt to crystallise some of the basic tenets of anti-racist social work as I see it. Given the nature of the subject matter, this attempt can be neither definitive nor comprehensive. The aim is to inform, raise consciousness and thus promote further study and debate rather than to provide 'the answer'.

1. The first step towards anti-racism is to recognise, and eradicate, our own racism. This is not a RAT-style guilt trip but an acknowledgement (in line with a PCS analysis) of the structural and cultural infuences on our behaviour and attitudes. If we are not sensitive to these issues, if we do not attempt to swim against the tide of racism, then we will be carried along by the strong current, knowingly or otherwise. Denney (1983) is therefore right to argue that: 'Above all is the importance of recognising racism in one's own practice. Failure to act against racism is in itself a form of unintentional or negative racism' (p. 172).

2. In recent years there has been considerable rhetoric about anti-racism and the notion of equal opportunities in general. There is therefore a danger that anti-racism remains at a rhetorical level only. It is much more comfortable for people to deal with it at this level without actually engaging with the issues. As Ahmad (1990) argues, anti-racist social work must be premised on more than just good intentions. There must be a real commitment to tackle some difficult and painful issues. The rhetoric is only of value if it is backed up by reality.

3. Social work with black and ethnic minority clients must operate on the basis of cultural *difference* and not *deficit*. All steps must be taken to ensure that assessment and intervention do not hinge on negative stereotypes – assumptions need to be checked out. The common ethnocentric tendency of pathologising black families, individuals or even whole communities is a very serious danger which must be avoided. For example, the ideological tendency to assume a higher level of criminality amongst black people (Gilroy, 1987, pp. 109–10; and Hall *et al.*, 1978) is a very destructive trap to fall into.

4. Following on from this is the need to help develop a positive black identity. This applies particularly to areas such as fostering and adoption (Haynes, 1986; and Small, 1989), although this remains a contentious area. The issue of a positive black identity is, however, a much wider one and would apply, for example, to social work with black elders (see Chapter 4). Maxime (1987) argues the point

strongly: 'one's identity is like the foundation stone of a building, if you don't have a solid foundation, you don't have a building at all' (quoted in Zacune, 1991, p. 43)

5. Affirmative action is a principle endorsed by Ahmad (1990) and she defines it in the following terms: 'Affirmative practice is not about discriminating in favour of Black clients and disfavouring white clients and "reversing discrimination". On the contrary, it is about condoning and ensuring equity in social work planning for practice' (p. 75). This involves recognising the accumulation of disadvantage black people have suffered as a result of racism and developing policies and practice which will help to overcome the difficulties this causes. Ignoring the need for affirmative action amounts to adopting a colour-blind approach.

6. Combating racism is not simply a matter of purging one's own practice of discriminatory elements. It involves challenging racist comments, actions or attitudes in others and creating anti-racist alliances. From a collective position it is then possible to tackle racist structures and institutional practices in social work agencies and, to some extent at least, in other social welfare and and related agencies. Setting out one's own anti-racist stall without seeking to influence others is a very narrow strategy with limited effectiveness.

7. In similar vein, it must be recognised that anti-discriminatory practice is not only the responsibility of practitioners but also of managers and educators. Managers have a role to play in setting an appropriate agenda, supporting staff through the difficulties of establishing and maintaining anti-racist social work (Woolfe and Malahleka, 1990) and so on. Similarly, social work educators have a crucial role to play in 'setting the context for change' (CD Project Steering Group, 1991) by helping workers and students understand the nature of racist oppression and help them to begin to develop stategies for combating it. Practitioners, in turn, have a part to play in supporting and encouraging such work on the part of managers and educators and to offer constructive criticism where appropriate.

8. As Ahmed (1991) argues, a strategy of 'permeation' is necessary. This means that issues of anti-racism should permeate policy, practice, management and training rather than be 'tagged on' as an additional consideration. Anti-racism should not be an optional extra but rather a fundamental dimension of our work. And this dimension needs to be linked to other important social divisions:

    > The task for all of us is to ensure that anti-racist strategies are not seen in isolation from other disadvantages and oppressions. Anti-racism has to be class-conscious. It has to be gender-conscious . . . but race, gender and class have not often been theorised about. The issue for social work is how to bring it all together in theory and practice. (Ahmed, 1991, p. 180)

9. A central feature of anti-discriminatory practice in general and anti-racism in particular is that of *empowerment*. This involves seeking to maximise the power of clients and to give them as much control as possible over their circumstances. It is the opposite of creating dependecy and subjecting clients to agency power. As we have seen, social work with black and ethnic minority clients, is characterised by an over-emphasis on controlling at the expense of caring and supporting. Empowerment entails reversing that trend by using social work skills and resources in ways which support service users in overcoming racism (see Ahmad, 1990, pp. 46–50).

10. The position of black workers employed in predominantly white organisations needs to be recognised. One common response has been that of 'dumping' (Dominelli, 1989b), that is, seeing anti-racism as the province of black workers. However, this can increase the sense of isolation and the pressure on black workers. Anti-racism must be a humanitarian endeavour in which black and white workers can work together to combat the oppression that black people – clients and colleagues – experience. Unless and until a supportive environment is created for black workers, the number of black social workers will remain low.

I hope that these ten points can help people in social work to take their thinking and their practice towards an anti-racist social work. They cannot, of course, provide formula answers but that is no bad thing. Moving away from formulas and stereotypes towards a more critical and informed approach is a basic tenet of anti-discriminatory practice.

Anti-racist social work is a complex area but this can be no excuse for failing to get to grips with the issues. As David Divine (1990) puts it:

> There must be an obligation on us all to support and help each other in a climate conducive to honest and humble exchange. There are no 'right on' answers and approaches. Once we acknowledge that fact, further progress can be made. (p. 14)

5

Ageism and Alienation

The terms 'sexism' and 'racism' have long been established in the English language and are not now seen as technical terms or jargon. The term 'ageism', however, is much less well established and, although being used more and more in social work and related disciplines, it is only just beginning to enter the vocabulary of everyday speech. This would seem to be a reflection of the lack of awareness of ageism and the questions it raises, and also an indication of its relatively low status as an area of study. This very fact is itself characteristic of ageism – the marginalisation of issues relating to age, particularly the *problems* of old age (Pitt, 1982).

Age is a social division; it is a dimension of the social structure on the basis of which power, privilege and opportunity tend to be allocated. Age is not just a simple matter of biological maturation, it is a highly significant social indicator. This is the case whatever our age – all ages are imbued with social significance – but as we shall see, old age has special consequences in terms of the attachment of meaning to life stages. The focus in this chapter is therefore on the social position of older people and what implications this has for social work with this client group.

With the major effects of demographic changes now being felt, social work with older people is attracting far more attention than has ever been the case in the past. With such a rapidly growing elderly population, demands for resources multiply to the extent that the skills of practitioners and managers are being severely tested. The pressure is on and is likely to rise for the foreseeable future. It is at precisely such times that corners may be cut and clients receive a less than

82

adequate service. In this way, older people can be vulnerable to bad practice due to demand for service far outstripping supply. When we consider that social work with older people has considerable discriminatory potential, there is a serious danger that overworked staff will inadvertently increase the degree of oppression experienced by older people. This situation adds even greater weight to the argument that a clear understanding of ageism and the foundations of anti-ageist practice should be a high priority for workers in this field. This chapter attempts to begin that process of understanding.

What is ageism?

By reiterating the definition of ageism by Fennell *et al.* (1988) in their seminal work on the sociology of old age: 'unwarranted application of negative stereotypes to older people' (p. 97), we can see close parallels with the views of Stevenson (1989) who covers similar ground by focusing on negative attitudes: 'The reasons for these attitudes are bound up with complex and profound forces . . . Unfounded prejudices and stereotyping are characteristics of ageist attitudes (p. 8). These definitions give the impression that ageism is located at the *P* level: personal prejudices and negative attitudes. In the case of Fennell *et al.*, this is misleading, as they also fully recognise the cultural and structural elements elsewhere in the text.

One of the earliest references to the concept of ageism would seem to be that of Butler (1975) and here the three levels or dimensions are acknowledged:

Ageism makes it easier to ignore the frequently poor social and economic plight of older people. We can avoid dealing with the reality that our productivity-minded society has little use for non-producers – in this case those who have reached an arbitrarily defined retirement age . . . Ageism is manifested in a wide range of phenomena, both on individual and institutional levels – stereotypes and myths, outright disdain and dislike, or simply subtle avoidance of contact; discriminatory practices in housing, employment and services of all kinds; epithets, cartoons and jokes. (p. 12)

Butler recognises the personal and institutional levels and relates the latter to structural issues such as productivity and the state-defined retirement age. The cultural level manifests itself in 'epithets, cartoons and jokes' as older people are frequently the objects of cruel humour – a reflection of their low status and the lack of respect accorded to them by dominant cultural values.

I shall focus later in this chapter on the structural dimension by considering the political economy approach of theorists such as Chris Phillipson. But for now the emphasis will be on the personal and cultural levels. In particular, I shall explore a number of common assumptions which both reflect and reinforce ageism. I shall expound each of these assumptions or 'equations' in turn.

Old equals useless This is the 'burden' model of old age. Older people are seen as 'past their best', no longer productive, no longer contributing to the economy and therefore a burden, a drain on the state's resources. This is often used as an excuse for not providing a service or for giving preferential treatment to younger people.

Old equals childlike Old age is often seen as a period of 'postadulthood' (Midwinter, 1990), almost a return to childhood. Older people can find they are having decisions made for them (for example, by professionals or relatives) without consultation, or their rights are being overlooked (Thompson, 1992b), or they are being patronised, for example, in the way they are referred to ('the old dear'). These are examples of what Leonard (1984) calls 'infantilisation', a process parallel to the demeaning tendency to refer to adult women as 'girls'.

Old equals not like children Paradoxically, older people are not treated like children in terms of protection or provision of services (Thompson, 1989). Social work with older people is often marginalised and treated as the 'poor relation' compared with more prestigious forms of practice such as childcare (Marshall, 1989).

Old equals ill As a general rule it is true that the greater one's age, the higher the incidence of illness will be. However, this is a long way from the commonly held assumption that all or even most older people are ill. Some people even think of old age as an illness. But, in reality, the extent of illness and infirmity in old age is grossly exaggerated (Qureshi and Walker, 1986, and Cameron *et al.*, 1989).

Old equals not ill Once again we have a paradox. When older people are genuinely ill (that is, they are not simply the victims of an ageist assumption) they often meet resistance and their symptoms can easily be dismissed with a comment such as: 'What do you expect at your age?' This is reflected in health service priorities as, for example, when old age is seen as a contraindication for some forms of treatment.

Old equals lonely Older people are often subjected to considerable pity as they are deemed to be 'lonely'. No doubt many older people are lonely, as indeed are many younger people. However, very many elderly people have a good social network and are not lonely. In addition, it is a mistake to equate being alone with being lonely. Whether someone is lonely or not needs to be assessed. To assume that an older person is lonely, without actually checking, is an ageist assumption.

Old equals asexual Sexuality in children tends to be discouraged and is seen as something 'reserved for adults'. However, following on from the second point above, it is significant that sexual activity amongst older people is often frowned upon or even seen as 'disgusting'. For example, an older man with a strong libido is described derogatively as a 'dirty old man' (de Beauvoir, 1977, p. 53) whereas his younger counterpart attracts more socially acceptable, albeit sexist, terms such as 'young buck'. Older people are thus denied their sexuality.

Old equals unintelligent Older people are often perceived as being less intelligent than younger people. There is often an implicit assumption that intellectual capacities are lower, if not significantly lower, for those people who have reached old age. This can be accompanied by an assumption that confusion is a 'normal' part of the ageing process. Thus older people are expected to be slow on the uptake and unable to understand complex issues. This, in turn, can lead to workers talking to them in an over-simplified, thus patronising way.

Old equals poor   As Phillipson (1989) argues, class differences tend to be magnified in old age and so poorer people may suffer considerable poverty when they reach old age. However, important though this is, we should not allow it to persuade us that old people, as a social group, are poor. Very many indeed are, but to begin one's assessment of an older person with the assumption that he or she is poor can lead to difficulties and could involve overlooking available solutions to presenting problems.

Old equals inhuman   There is a strong ideological tendency to dismiss older people, to deny them their humanity. I found a good example of this in an article in a newsletter of a local 'Alcohol Forum'. The author, a psychiatrist, is discussing safe limits for weekly alcohol consumption when he comments that: 'Safety limits are proposed in terms of alcohol units per week (10) but these limits are for males or females, not for the elderly'. Although the good intentions of the author are apparent elsewhere in the article, the common tendency to distinguish between 'ordinary people' (that is, males and females) and 'the elderly' is clearly in evidence.

This is not an exhaustive list and much more could be said on the topic. However, having gone some way towards clarifying what ageism is and what form it takes, let us now turn our attention to how these issues apply to social work.

The implications for social work

One manifestation of institutional ageism is the tendency for social work with older people to be seen as routine and uninteresting, and more suited to unqualified workers and social work assistants than to qualified social workers. For many staff, work with older people is seen as primarily matching service to need (and indeed the Griffiths Report and subsequent community care legislation tend to reinforce this – Kubisa, 1990).

It is relatively easy to focus on service provision without considering skills and methods of intervention. As I have argued elsewhere (Thompson, 1989), it is important to:

> ensure that social workers are allowed and encouraged to do social work with elderly people – to use social work methods. A truly anti-ageist practice would draw on a wide range of approaches and thus avoid making do with an almost mechanical matching of service to need. (p. ii)

Froggatt (1990) examines the family dimension of social work practice with elderly people. She acknowledges that the complexities of what she calls 'later life families' have been paid scant attention and it is only in recent years that studies of 'intergenerational caring relationships' have appeared (p. 6).

Ageism would have us disregard the family context and concentrate on service provision. But, as Froggatt explains:

> Elderly people are almost always in some sense part of a family with kin-related and social support networks. Any change in the vulnerable elderly person's capacity to cope with daily living should be considered in relation to his/her place in the family network, and the capacity of that network to respond to the change. (p. 18)

Thus the familial context of social work with older people needs to be borne in mind.

Ageism has two sets of implications for social work assessment. The first relates to the points raised above. That is, assessment needs to address not only simple notions of need and service availability but also wider issues which form part of a comprehensive assessment. The second relates directly to ageism and can be subdivided into two parts. On the one hand, assessment should include consideration of the impact of ageism on older people's lives, including, as we shall see below, low self-esteem, feelings of being a nuisance and so on. On the other hand, care needs to be taken to to ensure that ageist assumptions are not influencing the assessment work being undertaken. As with racism and sexism, if we are not actively 'swimming against the tide' of cultural and institutional ageism, we will be carried along with it, such is the strength of ageist ideology. Marshall (1989) makes a similar point when she argues that:

> Social work with elderly people is such an underdeveloped field of social work that it is littered with unchallenged, usually negative received ideas. These ideas are often not put into words but are carried into social work from society generally. They are to a large extent an expression of an ageist society. (p. 109)

Ageism therefore has major implications for assessment, and our awareness of ageism should flag up a number of dangers for us: assessment as a test of eligibility for service (Marshall, 1989, p. 112); assessment as primarily negative (Key, 1989) and so on. But ageism also applies to other aspects of social work. One major aspect of this is the danger of what Fennell *et al.* (1988) call 'welfarism', the tendency to focus on the 'needs' of older people in welfare terms, to pay scant attention to their *strengths* and, in so doing, exaggerate the extent of the problems experienced in old age.

This is applicable at two levels. In general terms, there is an often unspoken assumption that being old entails being in need of welfare services – but this needs to be balanced against the fact that only a relatively small proportion of people over retirement age receive Social Services assistance. More specifically, in relation to those older people who do become service users, welfarism can easily present them as a 'series of problems' rather than real people who have not only problems and needs but also strengths, assets and a positive contribution to make.

One implication of this is that oppressive ageist practices can actually be perpetuated by the good intentions of workers and general public alike who see a 'welfarist' approach to older people as kind and humane. The influence of ageist ideology ensures that the demeaning and patronising nature of welfarism is rarely realised by those who hold such views. As with anti-racism, good intentions alone are not enough. Indeed, welfarism shows that unenlightened good intentions can unwittingly reflect and reinforce ageist stereotypes.

Taking these issues a step further, Walker (1987) suggests that the desire to achieve 'nursing' status can lead to residential care staff increasing the dependence of the elderly people in their care: 'A long history of research shows suggests that the interests of the staff of residential homes are likely to tend towards the creation of dependency rather than independence amongst elderly residents' (p. 52). The word 'dependency' is an important one, as it is instrumental in creating a negative image of older people and gives credence to notions of older people as a nuisance or a burden. It is therefore vitally important that social work staff do not use the term loosely or uncritically.

Dependency implies physical frailty but Cameron *et al.* (1989) argue against the use of this misleading term 'frail elderly'. They point to the considerable inconsistency in the way the term is used and describe it as a 'service-led label' which excludes the client's own voice. Both terms, dependency and frailty, imply a medical model, one which focuses on physical capabilities and their decline or dysfunction. Such an approach runs the risk of oversimplifying the complex range of factors surrounding old age and reducing these to a medical or biological level. As Phillipson (1989) puts it:

> old age is being represented as a cluster of physiological and biological problems – the construction of dependency through economic and social inequality usually being ignored . . . terms such as 'frailty' and 'disability' are being used to stigmatize particular groups of older people and are being used to define service eligibility. (p. 198)

He goes on to argue the case for moving away from dependency towards 'interdependency'. This involves developing a partnership between service providers and service users in relation to service delivery and development.

Where independence is either not feasible or not desirable, the alternative should not be dependency based on the traditional paternalistic worker–client relationship. Rather, it should be interdependency which:

> provides recognition of the help older people need from us, as well as the rewards to be gained from giving this help . . . Most of

all, the idea of mutuality between young and old, worker and
older person, might offer social work practice the basis for a new
vision of how work with older people might be developed.
(Phillipson, 1989, p. 205)

The optimism inherent in this concept is to be welcomed,
especially in the context of a social work with older people,
which is often dismissed as routine and uninteresting or
reserved for unqualified staff (Thompson, 1992b). Social
work with older people is seen as less prestigious than, say,
childcare, and this in itself is a reflection of ageism, based on
the negative assumption that practice with older people
requires fewer skills and less application. Or, as Preston-
Shoot and Agass (1990) put it:

> dominant images of people's worth are acted out in service
> provision. Work with older people is seen as straightforward. It
> can wait. Child care is seen as complex and immediate. However,
> both require the same social work skills, present the familiar
> social work dilemmas and require sensitive handling of separa-
> tions, placements and culture. (p. 10)

Ageism also manifests itself in terms of the social policy
context and legislative framework. Matthews (1979) points
out that older people's needs are covered by the same
legislative and policy umbrella as disabled or infirm people,
thus indicating that such people are considered a homogeneous group – despite their varying needs and circumstances.
Policy in relation to community care can also be seen to
follow this pattern and reveal an assumption that there is no
need for a clear policy in relation to older people, as they can
be 'tagged on' to other policies.

Similarly, Marshall (1990) argues that the absence of
specific policy and legislation means that the protection
afforded to children is not available for older people as there
are no equivalent statutory requirements.

There is another sense in which older people are not
afforded the same protection as children. I am referring to
the phenomenon of old age abuse which is receiving increasing attention. As with child abuse, there is a problem in
establishing a precise definition of what constitutes abuse or

how the various forms should be categorised (Stevenson, 1989). However, this is not to deny the prevalence, significance or seriousness of such abuse. Older people can be physically or sexually abused, subjected to neglect (for those who are physically dependent on carers) and/or emotional abuse. These can be seen as a direct parallel with the abuse inflicted upon children.

However, there is an additional dimension as far as older people are concerned. Making decisions for children without consulting them may be considered by many as poor parenting but this would rarely be seen as child abuse. But in the case of elderly people this can be seen as an infringement of civil liberties and, as such, a form of abuse. This denial of citizenship can be linked directly to ageism (Thompson, 1992b) and, more specifically, to the notion of 'infantilisation' – the tendency to treat older people as if they were children. Social workers need to be wary of colluding with this by falling into the trap of listening to the carer(s) without hearing the voice of the older person.

The Centre for Policy on Ageing guide, *Community Life,* stresses the notion of partnership, not only between agencies but also between service users and service providers. Part of such a partnership is the key role of consultation: 'The code emphasises the value of consultation at all times. At all points in the process, consumers and carers should be consulted and have some influence on the services provided for them' (CPA, 1990, p. 36). Where such consultation routinely takes place, the risk to older people can be significantly reduced, as it makes elderly clients active participants rather than passive recipients. This helps to guard against the error of seeing carers as the 'parents' and thus in a position to make decisions on behalf of older people. It is only in a minority of situations (for example, where a carer holds Enduring Power of Attorney – see Norman, 1980, p. 3) that rights are vested in a carer.

But perhaps the most frequently reported abuse situation is more overtly harmful than a denial of rights – that is, direct physical abuse and/or mental cruelty by over-stressed and under-supported carers (Pulling, 1987). Ageism entails devaluing and marginalising older people, dismissing their contribution and their needs and presenting them as a burden or nuisance. The ageism inherent in social and economic policy leaves many older people and their carers as a low priority in terms of service provision. All this combines to give rise to a number of situations in which the stresses and tensions are increasingly likely to lead to abuse. Ageism is therefore a significant factor.

A further implication of ageism for social work is the way the oppression experienced by older people is internalised and manifests itself as low self-esteem. Marshall (1990) points out that, as with racism and sexism, the stereotypes of ageism can be internalised by those suffering discrimination. Indeed, it is not surprising that a group of people who are constantly receiving strong negative messages should perceive themselves in strongly negative terms. This has the effect of lowering morale and sapping confidence.

High self-esteem is premised on receiving positive messages, feeling valued and important, but, as we have seen, ageism acts as significant barrier to receiving such positive signals. Social work staff need to be sensitive to these issues in order to:

(a) avoid reinforcing negative and demeaning images; and
(b) seek opportunities to give positive feedback and enhance self-esteem.

A major component of successfully achieving high self-esteem is that of maintaining a thread of meaning to one's life – having targets to aim for and goals to achieve. As Simone de Beauvoir puts it: 'There is only one solution if old age is not to be an absurd parody of our former life, and that is to go on pursuing ends that give our existence a meaning' (p. 601). She then goes on to give examples of some possibilities: 'devotion to individuals, to groups or to causes, social, political, intellectual or creative work' (ibid.). She argues that our lives have value if we attribute value to the lives of others – through love, friendship, compassion or even indignation. These are important lessons for social workers and social care workers. Ageism would have us focus on 'care' and dependency. Anti-ageist practice would have us look to activity, meaning, value and esteem. The task is not to 'look after' but to motivate, empower and promote self-esteem.

Williamson (1979) captures this point well:

> it must be emphasised that care of the elderly is certainly not just a matter of giving them pensions and providing services for them. It involves the creation of a society in which old people are enabled to live their lives as they wish, in which they are enabled to retain positive and satisfying roles in which their self-esteem receives the kind of boosts and reinforcements which as human beings they require for their happiness and health. (p. 37)

Closely related to the notion of self-esteem is that of dignity. Dignity refers to the intrinsic worth of human beings and is therefore an important word in the anti-ageist vocabulary.

Set against this is the concept of 'risk', or more specifically protection from risk. Norman (1980) discusses a number of ways in which dignity and self-determination can be sacrificed in the name of protection from risk. In a later article she argues that 'an honest approach to the management of risk' should be part of a strategy in which improved professional practice can address issues of ageism (1987, p. 14).

Referring to the work of Brearley (1982) she comments on the need to understand risk as a matter of 'gambling' by weighing the dangers inherent in a particular situation against the potential benefits. She then goes on to clarify this by giving a concrete example:

> Does the physical safety of the move to live with a caring daughter or to residential care outweigh the psychological dangers of loss of independence? Does the danger to a daughter's health, earning power and family relationships outweigh the guilt and stress she feels in the present situation? (ibid., p. 15)

The balance of risk is an important aspect of social work with older people and, from the perspective of anti-discriminatory practice, we must be wary of allowing ageist ideology to tilt the balance in favour of an over-cautious, perhaps somewhat paternalistic, approach.

Ageism manifests itself at all three levels: personal, cultural and structural, and so the implications for social work staff reach far and wide. The development of anti-ageist practice therefore presents a major challenge for all concerned. I shall outline some of the steps towards anti-ageist practice later in this chapter. First, however, it is necessary to examine some of the arguments which have arisen in response to ageist ideology.

The anti-ageist response

Phillipson (1982) adopts a 'political economy' approach to understanding the position of older people in society. He comments as follows: 'I would argue that undue weight has been given to biological and psychological changes in old age (and the deterioration seen to accompany them), in contrast to the role played by the economic and political environment' (p. 2). He links negative attitudes towards older people to the structural requirements of the capitalist quest for profit. He argues that old age is seen as 'non-productive' and 'a period of social redundancy' (p. 7). But this is no coincidence – this negative and dismissive ideology is pervasive because it is linked inextricably with the economic requirements of capitalism.

Older people are seen as marginal to the labour market and are therefore assigned a lower status due to the emphasis on measuring social value in terms of one's contribution to the production of wealth. Old age therefore needs to be understood in economic and political terms. This structural approach is also evident in the works of Walker (1981, 1986, 1987) and, to a certain extent, Townsend (1981, 1986) as well as various other writers in the field of social gerontology. This has proved to be an influential approach that has tended to counterbalance the traditional perspective on old age which sees this life stage as predominantly a medical problem, as if old age were primarily a disease process (Haber, 1983).

Indeed, 'medicalisation' can be seen as an aspect of ageism, part of the social construction of old age as a *problem*. This medical perspective has had a major impact on the theory and practice of welfare professionals, as Fennell *et al.* (1988) argue:

> By the 1950s, then, a body of knowledge was available to respond to the needs of an ageing population. Crucially, however, much

of this knowledge was medically-inspired and orientated . . . But the influence of the medical perspective was adopted by other professions in the post-war period as they struggled to find an effective role with older people. Thus, for example, neither social work nor health visiting have built an independent knowledge base for work with this client group. (pp. 39–40).

Theorists who adopt a structural approach to old age are therefore keen to emphasise the social, political and economic determinants of the situation of older people. That is, they see old age as a period of 'structured dependency' which is socially constructed rather than biologically determined.

Bytheway and Johnson (1990) also argue that the essence of ageism lies in adopting a biological interpretation of the ageing process: 'Ageism is a set of beliefs originating in the biological variations between people and relating to the ageing process' (p. 36). They then go on to present what they see as four central pillars of an anti-ageist response:

1. Abandon ageist language. We should avoid grouping people together according to their age. Age should only be referred to when necessary. (See also Chapter 2 above for a discussion of ageist language.)
2. Recognise age for what it is:

    What is required is an assertion of personhood, a continuing personal sense of social identity and a popular acceptance of the realities of ageing. If it is argued, for example, that life is a continuing process of development and 'becoming', then this implies that age does matter and is valued. (p. 37)

3. Avoid the restrictions of chronological age. How old a person is should not be used as a stipulation (for example, in determining eligibility for a service). Individuals or groups should not be excluded from jobs, services, participation and so on purely on the grounds of age.
4. Abandon the 'us–them' mentality. We are all subject to the ageing process. We should be aware of this and therefore avoid separating off 'the old': 'the most damaging thing we can do – contributing immensely to the power of ageism – is to seemingly deny that "we" who

discuss these issues are somehow freed of the reality of the ageing experience' (p. 38).

In the same year that this article was published, the Church of England also added its weight to the development of anti-ageism. A report from the Board for Social Responsibility entitled simply 'Ageing' draws attention to the 'negative attitudes to ageing that are widespread in industrialised societies' (p. 140).

The report links ageism to two major factors and these are:

● fear of death; and
● a materialistic culture which equates success with productivity and economic activity.

It is these issues, the report contends, which lead to stereotypical negative attitudes towards older people and an undervaluing of their positive contribution to society. The report argues that the Church can play a more positive role in tackling ageism both within its own institutional structures and practices and in wider society as a whole. Also, in general social policy terms, a mixed economy of welfare approach is recommended, based on the view that a combination of private, voluntary and state services can best meet the needs of older people.

The role of the fear of death is one which also features in the work of de Beauvoir. In particular she questions the notion of death being near for older people:

> The old man knows that he will die soon; the fatality is as present at seventy as it is at eighty, and the word 'soon' remains as vague at eighty as it did at seventy. It is not correct to speak of a relationship with death: the fact is that the old man, like other men, has a relationship with life and nothing else. (p. 492)

In short, old age has more to do with life than it has to do with death. And this 'affirmation' of life is a key part of the existentialist philosophy on which de Beauvoir's work is based. But it is perhaps the other strand of her thinking, her seminal role in the development of feminism, which should interest us more here. For what we need to recognise is that ageism does not operate in isolation. It intersects with other forms of discrimination such as sexism and racism. These combinations of oppression are significant for social work practice and so they are worthy of closer attention.

Multiple oppressions

For demographic reasons the world of the old is predominantly a female world (Peace, 1986) as women far outnumber men in the later stages of life. The interrelationship of old age and gender therefore takes on a particular significance. Ford and Sinclair (1989) comment as follows:

> Women's experience of old age is both qualitatively and quantitatively different from that of men. While older people are subject to the discriminatory and demeaning processes of ageism, women suffer additional disadvantages because of their low status, their traditional role(s), their lack of economic power and because the majority of them live alone. (p. 74)

It is not simply a mathematical matter of adding sexism to ageism. The reality is much more complex than this. Older women will have a long and cumulative experience of sexism and will also have lived through a period of considerable change as far as social attitudes to women are concerned. The impact of sexism on older women and the effects of the interaction of sexism and ageism cannot therefore be routinely or straightforwardly predicted. These are *empirical*, rather than theoretical, matters; that is, they cannot be determined in advance, they need to be examined. There are, however, broad principles and characteristics which can be discerned.

Sontag (1978) described this combination of sexism and ageism as the 'double standard of ageing', a double disadvantage of discrimination. Victor (1987), in discussing these issues, argues that:

> Growing older is less problematic for a man because masculinity is associated with qualities such as competence, autonomy and self control. These valued attributes withstand the ageing process

much better than the qualities for which females are desired: beauty, physical attractiveness and childbearing . . . Later life is a time when men become grey-haired, distinguished, wise and experienced whilst women are typified as worn out, menopausal, neurotic and unproductive. (p. 96)

These are significant issues in relation to self esteem. Maintaining a degree of dignity and self-worth is more difficult for older women due to the structural and ideological constraints and this, in turn, can lead to a sense of 'postadulthood' and infantilisation as discussed earlier in this chapter.

Both these aspects, gender and age, also intersect with issues of race and ethnicity. Fenton (1987) points out that due to the earlier arrival in Britain of black men and their greater preponderance amongst post-war immigrants (at the height of the labour migration discussed in Chapter 2), there will be more black men than black women in the elderly population during the 1990s.

The Report of the Board for Social Responsibility (1990) also argues that:

> The special needs of elderly members of minority ethnic groups will become more important over the next few decades as the population ages and its profile becomes similar to that of the white population. One implication for policy making is the urgency of making sure that health and welfare services are sensitive to the needs of these groups. (p. 18)

And this sensitivity will also need to apply to the dimension of gender. Age, gender and race/ethnicity are fundamental aspects of our experience, and social work and social care practice needs to have least a basic understanding of these issues and how they interact in specific cases and particular contexts. And, as if this were not complex enough, we must also take account of the socioeconomic dimension – that of class. As has been noted, class differences in early life tend to be amplified in old age, thus accounting in part for the higher incidence of poverty amongst elderly people (Phillipson, 1989).

However, Norman (1985) takes matters a step further when she introduces the concept of 'triple jeopardy'. Mays (1983) had earlier described the combination of racism and ageism ('double jeopardy') as: 'the product of the accumulated experiences and problems of a lifetime of membership of a minority group, as well as the current experience of problems associated with old age' (p. 73). Norman took both these sets of issues (racism and ageism) and sought to understand them in relation to class – the physical and economic disadvantages associated with low socioeconomic position. The marginalisation resulting from low income is reinforced and extended by the additional discriminatory impact of both racism and ageism.

This triple jeopardy is an important element in the social context of ethnic minority elders. It therefore needs to feature in social work assessments and interventions and, on a wider scale, policies and service plans. Oppression is both a social injustice and a barrier to self-realisation and, as such, the removal, reduction and prevention of oppression are valid and legitimate aims for social work. Where two or more such oppressions combine or intersect their impact can be even more significant, and the resulting disempowerment even more far-reaching.

The point that this discussion reinforces is the need to adopt a holistic framework, an anti-discriminatory perspective which takes account not only of racism or sexism but also of ageism and disablism (and indeed the other forms of discrimination which will be exemplified in the discussions in Chapter 7). But this holistic framework must be applicable to actual practice if it is to be of value. The final section of this chapter addresses some of the key elements of putting such anti-discriminatory theory into practice.

Towards anti-ageist practice

Social work with older people has often been seen as low priority, relatively routine and undemanding work, although this view, in itself, is a reflection of ageist ideology and reveals a rather condescending (and misguided) attitude towards this area of work.

It is therefore important to be clear about what the social work task entails and how it can be achieved within the context of anti-discriminatory practice. It is therefore necessary to consider the steps necessary in order to move towards an anti-ageist practice. Some of these are outlined here.

1. Ageist stereotypes can easily seduce us into making negative assumptions about older people and thus establishing a framework for discrimination and oppression. Anti-ageist practice is therefore premised on avoiding and challenging ageist assumptions and myths. This is particularly important in relation the process of assessment. In fact, if we are not vigilant, assumptions can masquerade as assessment. The maxim should therefore be: **assess, don't assume!**

2. Much of the literature in relation to old age is from a medical perspective; old age is often presented as if it were a disease or pathological state. This has significant implications in terms of the construction of role expectations and attitudes. This, in turn, can have a major impact on self-image and thus on self-esteem. The ageism inherent in a medicalised approach to older people is a pitfall which social work must avoid. A key part of this is to cease using medical terminology in a social work context, for example, to speak of assessment and intervention rather than diagnosis and treatment.

3. Traditional social work is partly geared towards helping people 'adjust' to their personal and social circumstances. The problem with this is that it is: 'a "reductionist" approach insofar as it reduces a complex socio-psychological situation to a straightforward matter of pathology, of individual failing' (Thompson, 1991b, p. 16). Anti-ageist practice needs to transcend notions of 'adjustment' and focus instead on on *empowerment* – the development of older people's personal power and seeking ways of increasing it, for example, through advocacy or access to resources.

4. Townsend (1986) is critical of the welfare state's role in producing, or at least reinforcing, what he terms 'structured dependency'. Social welfare practice can play a part in constructing or increasing dependency in older people. It is therefore essential, in moving towards anti-ageist

practice, for social work to be active in avoiding depen-
dency-creation. We should aim for what Kuhn (1986)
calls 'interdependency' – the mutuality and human
affirmation involved in helping each other. As Phillipson
(1989) puts it:

> Fostering the idea of interdependency needs then, to become
> part of a new radical philosophy for work with older people.
> It provides recognition of the help older people need from
> us, as well as the rewards to be gained from giving this help.
> It also reminds us of the skills possessed by older people and
> the resources these might provide for activities and cam-
> paigns within the community. (p. 205)

5. Ageism marginalises older people and casts them in
secondary roles or presents them as useless and a burden
to society. In view of this, we should not be surprised if
many older people struggle to maintain a thread of
meaning or sense of purpose to their lives and thus fall
prey to low spirits or depression. In countering this,
V. W. Marshall's notion of 'authorship' should be a
useful part of the anti-ageist social worker's repertoire.
It is a concept akin to empowerment – having a sense of
being in control of one's life, and, as Marshall stresses, of
one's death: 'if people want their lives to be meaningful
stories with good endings, they also want to be the
authors. This is the taking of responsibility for one's
life as a whole, including its ending in death' (1986a,
p. 142). Social work staff must not shy away from issues
of death or dying for these are part of life, of meaning
and of personal responsibility.

6. Ageism, as with other forms of oppression and discrimination, is both reflected in, and constructed by, language.
Anti-ageist social work therefore needs to be sensitive to
the role of language and thus avoid ageist and depersonalising terms such as 'the elderly'. We should always
remember to add the word 'people', that is, 'elderly
people', or better still 'older people'. The term 'elders'
is also a positively valued one, especially as it has
connotations of respect and dignity. Social work staff
often use demeaning and perhaps patronising terms to

refer to their older clients but do so in good faith without realising their negative impact. Examples of this would be: 'old dears', 'my old darlings' and so on. What is needed, therefore, is a greater sensitivity to language so that it can become a tool of anti-ageism rather than a sign of unchallenged ageism.

7. The effectiveness and appropriateness of services offered and work undertaken will depend in large part on the quality of the assessment which establishes the framework for intervention. It is therefore important that such assessment should be *holistic* – taking account of a wide range of factors. The trap which lures many an unsuspecting worker is the routine matching of service to need. This is an 'off the peg' approach in which the complex process of assessment is reduced to checking eligibility for services available. This latter approach is too narrow and restrictive in its scope and has no impact on service development. It has no place in a genuinely anti-ageist practice.

8. Ageism has the effect of undermining a sense of dignity and the self-esteem which partly depends on it. Ageism marginalises, excludes and demoralises. A key task within a programme of developing anti-ageist practice must therefore be the promotion of dignity and the enhancement of self-esteem – a counterbalance to the prevalence of negative stereotypes. In effect, this is not a single task, but rather an aspect of all the tasks undertaken in work with older people – an essential dimension or underlying principle of all our dealings with older people.

9. One significant aspect of ageist ideology is the process of infantilisation – treating older people as if they were children. This manifests itself in relation to the question of taking risks. Social work has followed the medical profession in adopting a rather protective approach to this issue. As Norman (1987) puts it: 'we deny them, as we deny children, the right to take responsibility for their sexuality, their behaviour and their risk-taking' (p. 14). In recognising this we must also recognise that the more protective we become the more we challenge older people's rights to make their own decisions and be

responsible for themselves. Anti-ageist practice needs to ensure that the protection offered is not at the expense of rights.
10. Anti-ageism is not a separate area of practice. It needs to be seen in relation to sexism (as the vast majority of older people are women) and racism (as the number of older black people is increasing significantly). These are fundamental aspects of human experience and need to be understood in relation to each other. Anti-ageism needs to be part of the wider enterprise and challenge of anti-discriminatory practice. The lessons learned from anti-racism and anti-sexism must also be applied to anti-ageism. They are not in conflict or competition but rather part of the wider movement towards an emancipatory social work.

These are all important steps towards putting anti-ageism firmly on the social work agenda and, moreover, making it a reality in day-to-day practice.

6

Disability and Social Handicap

The field of social work with disabled people is a long-established one but it is only relatively recently that the basis of this work has been seriously questioned and challenged. The old assumptions and certainties are no longer intact and and a very different approach to issues of disability is now emerging.

The development of the Disabled People's Movement has introduced a new, politicised approach to meeting the needs of disabled people, an approach which is highly critical of traditional perspectives on this area of social work practice. This new approach is based on a social – rather than medical or psychological – model of disability and, as we shall see in more detail below, this entails quite a significant shift in how disability is to be perceived, understood and acted upon.

Social work with disabled people has never achieved a priority status and has to a large extent been marginalised as a minority special interest, often receiving minimal attention on professional qualifying courses. It has also often been subsumed within medical discourse and seen as a paramedical undertaking somewhat distanced from mainstream social work (in parallel with health-related social work). It is thus given low status, low levels of funding and relatively little attention in terms of research and professional development.

This state of affairs can itself be seen as discriminatory and indicative of the marginalised and negatively valued position of disabled people and issues concerned with their wellbeing. This is illustrative of what has become known as *disablism*, systematic discrimination and prejudice against people with disabilities that produces a milieu of oppression and degradation.

What is disablism?

Disablism is a relatively new concept to be introduced into social work literature. Like ageism, however, it is steadily gaining ground and achieving greater currency. This is important as the issues cannot be confronted and problems resolved until they are firmly on the agenda. To do this we need the vocabulary, we need to name the enemy we are fighting in order to recognise it and muster our resources against it.

Disablism is therefore an important term even if the introduction of another 'ism' does seem trite and could lead some less sensitive souls to dismiss it as an academic fad. Disablism refers to the combination of social forces, cultural values and personal prejudices which marginalises disabled people, portrays them in a negative light and thus oppresses them. This combination encapsulates a powerful ideology which has the effect of denying disabled people full participation in mainstream social life. Disablism therefore incorporates an undermining of citizenship, a point to which I shall return in more detail below.

Disablism shares many of the features of ageism: a tendency towards infantilisation, a patronising 'does she take sugar?' attitude, an assumption of illness and so on. Indeed Phillipson's (1982) analysis of the political economy of ageing also provides a framework for understanding the political economy of disability, as the discussion of the work of Finkelstein (1981b), later in this chapter, will show.

This can be linked to the PCS model of discrimination as disablism can be seen to operate at all three levels: *P* – personal prejudice against disabled people is relatively commonplace and manifests itself in attitudes of revulsion, dismissiveness and – paradoxically – also in misplaced charitable concern in which dignity and human rights are exchanged for patronage and good deeds. (This argument will be pursued more fully below.) *C* – cultural values reflect various responses to disability and disabled people, but they are primarily negative in their orientation. Dominant cultural norms are geared towards the able-bodied majority and popular notions present disabled people as either misfits or pathetic victims of personal tragedy. They are also subject to abusive and derogatory treatment in jokes and other forms of humour. *S* – 'differential ability' is rarely recognised in sociology texts as a dimension of social stratification and yet it very clearly acts as a social division. This is manifested in the way public services and buildings are provided for the 'general public' but often without due regard for their appropriateness for disabled people, for example, in terms of access or other facilities. Thus, disabled people are structurally/institutionally defined as a marginalised social group; that is, they are not seen as part of the 'general public'.

Oliver (1990) links disablism to the workings of capitalism, the role of wage labour and the pursuit of profit. These are structural factors which underpin the cultural and personal dimensions of disablism and the ideology that sustains them, as we shall see below in the section on the response of the Disabled People's Movement.

PCS analysis is therefore no less applicable to disablism than to the other forms of discrimination and oppression discussed in earlier chapters. One manifestation of disablism is to see disability as a personal tragedy and to focus at the individual level without considering the wider issues of how current social arrangements systematically marginalise and disempower disabled people. Ann Shearer (1981) argues that the focus should be less on how disabled people can or should adjust to their impairment and more on how society can adjust to the needs of disabled people: 'How far is society willing to adjust its patterns and expectations to include its members who have disabilities, and to remove the handicaps that are now imposed on their inevitable limitations?' (p.10).

These comments form the basis of a social model of disability which is based on a fundamental distinction between impairment and disability. The Union of the Physically Impaired Against Segregation (UPIAS, 1976) defines the two terms as follows:

Impairment lacking part or all of a limb, or having a defective limb, organ or mechanism of the body;

Disability the disadvantage or restriction of activity caused by a contemporary social organisation which takes no or little account of people who have physical impairments and thus excludes them from the mainstream of social activities. (pp. 3–4)

On this basis the Derbyshire Coalition of Disabled People, a key group in the development of the Disabled People's Movement in Britain, define disability in social rather than individual terms:

We hold that disability is caused by segregative social arrangements which deny equality of opportunity for impaired people to participate in mainstream social activities. We are committed to the removal of all such barriers, whether physical, organisational or attitudinal and their replacement by arrangements which enable us to play a full part in the social, political and economic life of the county. (DCDP Equal Opportunities statement, 1986)

This raises a number of issues for social work staff – are they to be seen as part of the struggle to remove such barriers or are they themselves barriers and obstacles due to the tradition of individualism inherent in conventional approaches to disability? This is a question which will recur in some of the later discussions within this chapter.

To see disability as a matter of personal tragedy or pathology is, to use Ryan's (1971) concept, an example of 'blaming the victim'; that is, the wider social and political dimensions are ignored and the focus remains on a narrow, individualistic level. What is needed, therefore, is a social model of disability or, more specifically, a social oppression model, as this is consistent with the principles of anti-discriminatory practice. Such a model will be explored in more detail in the 'Disabled People's Movement' section below.

A social model of disability underpins the concept of disablism, the meaning of which Oliver (1989b) defines as follows:

The rise of the disabled people's movement and, especially, its re-definition of the problems of disability as social oppression has given rise to the concept of disablism, which simply means any ideas or practices which contribute to the oppression of disabled people rather than their emancipation. The individual model of disability, both as a set of ideas and as a basis for practice, is itself disablist in that it furthers the existing oppression of disabled people. (p. 21)

The movement from an individual conception of disability to a social one has many implications for social work and it is to these that we now turn.

The implications for social work

Traditionally, social work with disabled people has a major practical emphasis, with a focus on matching available services to assessed need. In this respect there is a strong parallel with traditional social work with older people, as discussed in the previous chapter. Oliver (1983) is critical of such an approach, which fails to question what is meant by 'need' and also whether the services on offer are appropriate. He comments: 'If only social work with people with disabilities were as simple as this practical approach implies – the matching of resources to needs within a legal and statutory framework' (p. 3). This in itself can be seen as indicative of disablism in so far as it fails to see disability as a social and political issue, and reduces it to a matter of the welfare state providing services for 'dependent' people – thus socially constructing disability as a form of dependency. The 'practical' approach can therefore be understood as an additional form of social oppression that is instrumental in constructing an image of disabled people as helpless and not able to contribute to mainstream society.

This also has implications for those who care for disabled people, as it casts them in a role which can so easily reinforce notions of dependency and pathology. The dominant disablist ideology can have the effect of allowing and encouraging carers to contribute unwittingly to the oppression of the people they are, in most cases, genuinely trying to help.

What all this means is that social workers adopting an anti-discriminatory perspective cannot afford to settle for a 'practical' approach with an uncritical conception of need. Service delivery must therefore be based on a more sophisticated understanding of the notion of need and the related concept of *aiding*. What is often overlooked in relation to 'aids to daily living' is the degree of reliance on such aids by 'able-bodied' people. How many could lead 'normal' lives without everyday aids such as pens, cars, telephones, watches, cutlery, reading glasses, stairs and so on? There exists for each of us a 'structure of aiding', a set of practical and human support systems which enable us to pursue our day-to-day tasks and lifestyle. For a person with an impairment, the structure of such aiding will be different from that of a non-impaired person. However, this is a very different proposition from stating that disabled people need 'aid' (and, by implication, that non-disabled people do not).

The reality of the situation is that all people need some form of assistance or support to participate in mainstream social life. We all have our own requirements, some of which will be common to all, some of which are more individually tailored. However, the way in which such assistance is resourced is a significant issue. For example, government funding is provided in grants and services for individuals and groups, including business interests, and for the general public. That is, aiding is not only for those 'in need'. In fact, the majority of government funding is provided for groups other than people deemed to be 'in need'. It is therefore inappropriate, and indeed stigmatising, to see the needs of disabled people as 'special', as this draws an arbitrary line between those with an impairment and those without (Shearer, 1981). To see aid as something disabled people need but others do not is itself disabling, and indeed disablist. Traditional social work approaches to disability therefore run the risk of falling into this trap.

Oliver (1987) goes a step further by questioning the traditional helper–helped relationship (see also Finkelstein, 1981a; and Davis, 1988):

> I would further criticise the 'professionalisation' of service for disabled people, on the assumption that the professionals know best what disabled people need and are in charge. The provision of services in such a way is at best patronising, and at worst

further disabling, since disabled people may be pushed into becoming passive recipients of the kinds of services other people think they ought to have. (Oliver, 1987, p.18)

What is needed, therefore, is a social work which focuses on partnership rather than paternalism and which sees disabled people not as dependent or childlike but as an oppressed group who are denied the assistance they need, whilst assistance for other groups is freely provided.

An example of this would be access to public buildings such as libraries. Steps, where needed, would be provided as a matter of course, whereas a ramp for wheelchair access would be regarded as a 'special' requirement and may therefore be denied on the grounds of cost. In this way, disabled people may be excluded from libraries and other public buildings.

This has a major impact in terms of citizenship and rights. The citizenship of disabled people is undermined by the process illustrated in Figure 6.1, which also shows that it is not the impairment itself that is disabling but rather the social forces which exclude, marginalise and oppress. The handicap is therefore social rather than physical. This places social workers in a pivotal position within the context of the 'care versus control' dilemma so characteristic of the profession and its undertakings. On the one hand, social work practice can reinforce the traditional individualist model:

The individual model sees the problems that disabled people experience as being a direct consequence of their disability. The major task of the professional is therefore to adjust the individual to the particular disabling condition. There are two aspects of this: first there is physical readjustment through rehabilitation programmes designed to return the individual to as near normal a state as possible; and second, there is psychological adjustment which helps the individual to come to terms with physical limitations. (Oliver, 1983, p. 15)

The dangers of such a narrow, individualistic approach to social work have already been exemplified in earlier chapters. These include:

● A tendency to 'pathologise', to see the problem as being within the client/service user;

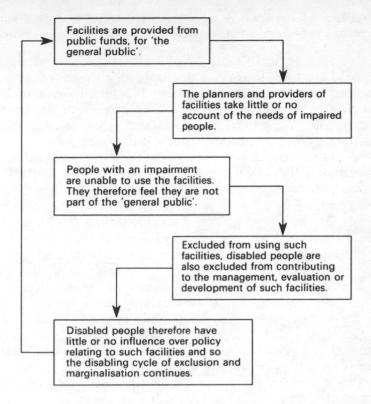

Figure   6.1

● A tendency to ignore wider cultural and structural factors; and
● Taken-for-granted discriminatory assumptions are not questioned.

In short, it reintroduces many of the weaknesses in theory and practice that radical social work sought to remove.

On the other hand, social work practice can confront, challenge and debunk the discriminatory and oppressive basis of the individualist model. Oliver (1983) echoes Finkelstein's (1981b) view that the real problem is:

one of the need for a change in professional role – the professional must change in role from expert definer of need and/or rationer of services and become a resource which the disabled person may use as he or she chooses. (p. 128)

A key element in this change is a movement away from a medicalised social work with disabled people towards a practice premised on empowerment. This entails social workers aligning themselves with the Disabled People's Movement and moving away from the traditional ethos of many disability organisations which:

> create and reinforce negative stereotypes of disability, referring to the 'tragedy of disability' or using demeaning imagery. The movement is trying to establish a disability culture to emphasise empowerment and pride, to create services run by disabled people themselves. (George, 1991, p. 21)

Brisenden (1986) is also critical of a medicalised approach to disability and argues that the emphasis on clinical diagnosis leads to a 'partial and inhibiting view of the disabled individual' (p. 173). Indeed, this is characteristic of the 'medical model' in general – a perspective which takes one aspect of a complex whole and presents it as a major or primary focus (see Oliver, 1990, for a fuller analysis of how this applies in the case of disability).

A medical model is not only unhelpful through presenting too narrow and negative a picture of disabled people, it also succeeds in relocating power and control in the hands of professionals, specifically medical professionals. This, in turn, plays a significant part in the social construction of dependency. Finkelstein (1991) also regrets the dominance of the medical model but sees it as part of a wider model, which he terms the 'social death' model of disability, referring to the work of Miller and Gwynne (1972). These two researchers likened the institutionalisation of disabled people to a form of 'social death' but, sadly, their response to this was not to challenge this fundamentally but rather to make such a 'death' as humane and efficient as possible.

Finkelstein (1991) criticises Miller and Gwynne for adopting: 'the simplistic assumption that to be permanently disabled means that the individual is *intrinsically* non-equal to their peers (i.e. without help, a non-being)' (p. 26). Their model is a profoundly discriminatory one, which banishes disabled people to a marginally less than human existence. As with the other forms of discrimination discussed in earlier chapters, the fact that the oppression experienced derives from misguided good intentions is of little comfort to those affected.

What emerges from these narrow perspectives is an image of disabled people as individuals for whom a 'cure or care' approach is appropriate. No account is taken of human rights, equality, independence or empowerment. These are all conveniently brushed to one side. It is clear, therefore, that an anti-discriminatory social work practice with disabled people must avoid the dangers of accepting a medical definition of disability or a conception of disabled people as 'socially dead'. The focus of practice must not be on the presumed inadequacies of disabled people but on the personal, cultural, structural and physical barriers to taking control of one's own life as far as possible – in short, a social work of empowerment. A significant aspect of this is a shift of focus from charity and compassion to advocacy and rights. As Oliver (1990) argues, social policies, including social work itself, should be geared towards alleviating oppression rather than 'compensating' disabled people for their 'tragedy'.

The question of the rights of disabled people is one which has received relatively little attention from social workers, or indeed from the state:

> The 1980s have seen a further retreat from the notion of rights as a result of policy makers' preference for voluntary rather than statutory services. And while the introduction of the 1986 Disabled Persons (Services, Consultation and Representation) Act promised meaningful collaboration between service users and providers, there is widespread disregard for the law by local authorities. (Barnes, 1991a)

One factor which can partly explain this disregard for the law and, by extension, the rights of disabled people, is the contradiction between the rights model implicit in this legislation and the medical model which underpins the majority of policy and practice in social work agencies. Whilst a medicalised individualist view remains dominant, the emphasis will continue to be on 'adjustment' and treatment rather than on empowerment, participation and rights.

Davis (1988) takes this a step further by arguing that there is a need to change focus so that resources are diverted to dealing with the social causes of disability rather than seeking to deal with the effects. A movement away from a medical model to a social model is a key part of this:

> The influence of this 'medical model' permeates much post-war legislation affecting disabled people. The growth of vested interests in segregated homes, day centres and transport, of sheltered workshops and special schools is an unavoidable aspect of this approach. On the other hand, a 'social model' of disability would stimulate structural change. It would, for example, tend to focus resources on changes in the way trans- port systems, employment practices and the built environment were designed and organised. (p. 13)

The current emphasis on 'care management' as a key part of the development of community care also retains the influence of the medical model, for example in the assumption that the professional experts know best what the needs of disabled people are. Oliver (1989c) is critical of the care management approach exemplified by Hunter (1988), which assumes that the disabled person cannot be his or her own care manager.

Anti-disablist practice therefore clearly entails dismantling the traditional medicalised approach and constructing, in its place, a social work practice premised on a social oppression model of disability.

The development of the 'independent living' paradigm (de Jong, 1979) offers social workers a way forward in tackling many of these issues. It focuses on achieving independence and achieving maximisation of an individual's potential. It mainly manifests itself in the establishment of Centres for Independent Living. Basically, such centres examine ways in which policies and services can be changed or created to facilitate maximum independence.

Centres for Independent Living were introduced in the USA in the early 1970s. In the mid-1980s a similar centre was established in Britain, at Ripley in Derbyshire, but with a slightly different focus. The Derbyshire centre is known as a

Centre for *Integrated* Living and constitutes a partnership between local disabled people and the statutory service providers. At its inception the centre aimed to provide a range of services:

1. Maintenance of and updating the Disabled Persons Register.
2. Setting up a county-wide care attendant register.
3. Housing services, from design to direct labour.
4. A co-ordinated, county-wide accessible transport service.
5. Mixed physical ability, commercially viable workshops.
6. Information, advice and associated support services.
7. Publicity and communications service.
8. Aids and equipment showroom and store.
9. 'Halfway House' rehabilitation service.
10. Peer counselling service. (DCDP, 1985)

This gives an outline of the thinking behind establishing the centre and can act as a model for other areas to follow in seeking an anti-discriminatory approach to social work with disabled people. Such centres can facilitate what Oliver (1987) sees as an important policy goal:

> At the organisational level [Social Services] departments must be prepared to develop partnerships with groups of disabled people, to employ disabled people as service providers and to involve them at all levels in committees, planning groups and working parties. (p. 19)

Amongst the key elements of such an approach is a greater control by disabled people themselves over their lives and circumstances. But it must be recognised that poverty acts as a major limitation on such control. Without the financial wherewithal to build an independent lifestyle, people with an impairment will remain, to a certain extent at least, *dis*-abled victims of a social/political handicap rather than a physical one.

Doyal (1983) recognises a twofold relationship between poverty and disability. On the one hand, disability consigns impaired people to a position of low income and, on the other hand, 'poverty is itself a major cause of disability' (p. 7, quoted in Oliver, 1990) (see also Borsay, 1986). The links between disability and the economy will be discussed in the following section but the point to note at this stage is the significance of poverty as a restrictive factor in the lives of disabled people. This places issues of welfare rights advocacy on the social work agenda, along with steps towards improved employment opportunities (Simpkin, 1981; and Lynes, 1974).

Again, the question of rights arises and this is indeed a major issue for anti-disablist social work – the development of an approach in which strategies of intervention address rights, integrated living and participation rather than adjustment or rehabilitation. This involves challenging discriminatory and oppressive structures, practices and attitudes both within and outside social work organisations.

Unlike issues of race and gender where anti-discrimination legislation exists – however limited its scope and impact – there is no equivalent legislation, in Britain at least. The British Council of Organisations of Disabled People (BCODP) is at the forefront of campaigning for such legislation (Barnes, 1991b; and Bynoe, Oliver and Barnes, 1991), and social workers committed to anti-discriminatory practice would do well to consider adding their weight to calls for such a legislative framework to act as a springboard for the further development of anti-discriminatory policy and practice.

The anti-disablist response – the Disabled People's Movement

'The Disabled People's Movement' is a generic term used to describe the politicisation of disability issues and the constriction and consolidation of an approach which avoids, and indeed undermines, the traditional model of disability. The movement promotes, as we have seen, a model of disability as a form of social oppression rather than personal misfortune or 'tragedy':

> This oppression ranges from the attitudes of able bodied individuals, to an environment which is largely inaccessible, to institutions.

The latter includes charities run by able bodied people who think disabled people need things done for them, the medical profession which keeps disabled people as sick people, and above this, the lack of any anti-discrimination legislation to give disabled people some protection. (Webb, 1989a, p. 18)

This passage aptly summarises some of the main areas addressed by the Disabled People's Movement, the various dimensions of oppression experienced by disabled people but rarely, if ever, acknowledged by traditional approaches to disability.

Borsay (1986) argues that a significant degree of oppression and inequality derives from the segregated nature of social services provision that arises from an individualistic policy model which seeks to accommodate disabled people to 'normal society' rather than construct a society which does not marginalise or exclude disabled people.

The individualist approach which constructs disability as a matter of personal tragedy is a model the Disabled People's Movement seeks to replace with a more politically informed strategy for, as Oliver (1986) argues, the traditional approach leaves 'social and economic structures untouched' (p. 16). Finkelstein (1981b) links disability with social and political factors by tracing the historical development of the role of impaired people in the economy. Prior to the Industrial Revolution people with an impairment were able to contribute to production in cottage and family-based industries as machines were relatively simple and easily adapted. Modern industrial methods, however, are less easily adapted, are located away from the home and involve a division of labour, thus excluding significant numbers of impaired people from the labour market and thus from the opportunity to be financially self-sufficient. Dependency is therefore caused not by the impairment itself but by the social arrangements which take no account of the needs of people with an impairment.

Oliver (1990) adopts a similar line of argument in linking the exclusion of disabled people to the workings of capital. He contends that there are both economic and ideological reasons for capitalist social relations to marginalise disabled people. Economically, they contribute to the 'reserve army of labour' in much the same way as women, ethnic minorities and older people. That is, disabled people provide the capitalist economy with a degree of flexibility in managing fluctuations in the demand for labour. Ideologically, the inferior position of disabled people serves 'as a warning to those unable or unwilling to work' (p. 70).

There are therefore structural reasons for the inequitable position of disabled people in Western society; it is no coincidence or historical accident – it is, in part at least, the outcome of historic material forces not unconnected with the nature of the capitalist economic system and the ideology of competitiveness and individualism which sustains it. This ideology is instrumental in constructing disabled people in negative terms, as people with problems – or even as people who *are* problems. Thus this dominant ideology of disability focuses specifically on the negative aspects of impairment and thereby presents a biased and unbalanced picture of disabled people. As Abberley (1987) puts it:

> As in the cases of women and black people, oppressive theories of disability systematically distort and stereotype the identities of their putative subjects, restricting their full humanity by constituting them only in their 'problem' aspects. (p. 16)

It is precisely this negative, demeaning and thus discriminatory, perspective on disability that the Disabled People's Movement is determined to fight and ultimately eliminate. The dehumanisation inherent in disablism is an important target for the attentions of those committed to achieving equality of opportunity and human rights.

Such dehumanisation manifests itself in the language used to describe, or refer to disabled people, as Brisenden (1986) indicates in the following passage:

> To begin with, we are not 'the disabled'. We are disabled people or even people with disabilities. It is important that we do not allow ourselves to be dismissed as if we all come under this one great metaphysical category 'the disabled'. The effect of this is a depersonalisation, a sweeping dismissal of our individuality, and a right to be seen as people with our own uniqueness rather than

the anonymous constituents of a category or group. These words that lump us all together – 'the disabled', 'spina bifida', 'tetraplegic', 'muscular dystrophy' – are nothing more than terminological rubbish bins into which all the important things as people get thrown away. (p. 174)

This powerfully-worded statement captures well the impact an ill-considered use of language can have on disabled people. A key factor in the struggle against disablism is therefore the development of a greater sensitivity to the discriminatory effects of language and the construction of a more appropriate vocabulary of empowerment.

Much work remains to be done before equality of opportunity can become a reality for disabled people. The 'charitable' approach, which presents disabled people as objects of pity and sympathy, has a long history and so its influence and consequences will not wither away overnight. This is especially the case when we consider that this approach has not developed in isolation but is, rather, a reflection of the broader economic and political sphere which values people's contribution to society in terms of the part they play in the production process and the creation of wealth.

It is partly in recognition of these wider aspects that the Disabled People's Movement has sought to politicise disability issues by, for example, seeing them as a civil rights matter, a struggle for the replacement of charity with rights, rather than simply a call for more or better services. We are witnessing what de Jong (1979), referring to the work of Kuhn (1962), calls a 'paradigm shift'. What is called for is not a modification of the existing approach or 'paradigm', but rather a completely new paradigm that focuses not on individual tragedy or 'special' needs but more appropriately on the barriers to empowerment and self-realisation that a disabling society places before those citizens who have an impairment.

The Disabled People's Movement seeks to reconstruct the image of disabled people in the eyes of mainstream society. They seek to establish the recognition that *all* people require some form of aiding to live satisfactory day-to-day lives and we should not discriminate against impaired people simply because the aiding they require is different from that needed

by the majority (that is, different *not* special). It is an arrogant
and inaccurate assumption to see disabled people as those in
need of aid, as opposed to able-bodied people who are not.

This more radical approach casts down a considerable
challenge to social workers as the actions of social work
staff cannot be neutral – they will either follow traditional
lines and thus reinforce the oppression of disabled people or
they will challenge traditional methods by contributing to the
emancipation and empowerment of people with disabilities.

Multiple oppressions

So far in this chapter the emphasis has been specifically on the
oppression inherent in the social response to disability. The
aim of this section, then, is to widen the focus somewhat in
order to consider how disablism intersects with other forms of
discrimination and oppression. This is, of course, a complex
and multi-faceted area and so, once again, it must be
recognised that the discussion here is exploratory and far
from comprehensive.

Disablism has a particular link with ageism as the incidence
of impairment is greater in the older age groups than in the
population as a whole. This statistical point is often miscon-
strued and it emerges as an aspect of ageist ideology: the false
assumption that old age itself is a form of disability or
impairment (see Chapter 5). However, what does, in fact,
occur is that very many older people suffer the dual oppression of a combination of ageism and disablism; they are
marginalised and negatively stereotyped on both counts. This
can have the effect of amplifying the discriminatory impact of
both forms of oppression. An example of this would be
attitudes towards sexuality. As has been noted in Chapter 5,
ageism constructs older people as asexual and thus presents
sexual activity in old age as 'deviant'. A similar process occurs
in relation to disabled people, who are also assumed to be
asexual. A disabled older person therefore faces an even
greater attitudinal barrier to fulfilling sexual desire.

Many other examples could be given but I hope the point is
clear that age and disability are not simply separate social

forces – they converge and overlap in many significant ways that will have important implications for older disabled people. One result of this is that social workers who work with older people should be conscious not only of issues of ageism but also of disablism.

Gender also features as a significant dimension of the experience of disabled people. Lonsdale (1990) covers many aspects of the complex intertwining of gender and disability and she explores a number of important themes. One such theme is that of dependency:

> Dependency has particular implications for women because of the important part which gender plays in determining whether someone is expected or encouraged, or indeed is even allowed to be independent. Since women are encouraged to play a more dependent role in society than men, women with disabilities often have a particular struggle to achieve control over their own destinies, although they are sometimes 'allowed' out of the passive and dependent female role. (pp. 10–11)

Social expectations of dependency apply to women in general within the strictures of patriarchy, but for disabled women the additional stereotyped equation of disability with dependency further promotes an image of disabled women as people who need to be 'looked after'. It does not then take much imagination to see the impact of of this as negative and limiting. Similarly, Lonsdale argues that women are 'invisible' in the majority of accounts of disability and so issues of gender and sexism are not paid adequate attention even though far more women than men have disabilities.

One account which does recognise the intersection of sexism and disablism is that of Oliver (1990). Drawing on the work of Brittan and Maynard (1984) he discusses the 'ideology of masculinity' and the limited responses to disablement available to men and women. That is, he recognises the way in which patriarchy seeks to predefine roles for both men and women and links this to specific issues of disability. Gender roles take on an extra significance from the standpoint of disability and place extra pressures and restrictions on disabled women in particular. He illustrates this by quoting Fine and Asch (1985):

Whereas disabled men are obliged to fight the social stigma of disability, they can aspire to fill socially powerful male roles. Disabled women do not have this option. Disabled women are perceived as inadequate for economically productive roles (traditionally considered appropriate for males) and for the nurturant, reproductive roles considered appropriate for females. (p. 5)

Oliver describes this as a 'double disability' which compounds the oppression of the negative social response to impairment. Thus disabled women are seen as 'roleless' and 'lacking in opportunities for self affirmation' (Fine and Asch, 1985, p. 9). In short, sexism amplifies the negative effects of disablism.

Lonsdale (1991), however, offers some hope that the emergence of a new approach to disability can improve the situation for disabled women. She comments:

Women with disabilities, therefore, stand to gain considerably from a politics of disability that encourages assertiveness and independence and aims to put the control of social service provision back in the hands of the recipient. (p. 15)

A social work of empowerment is also a relevant issue in considering how disability and race combine to provide another example of interlocking and mutually reinforcing oppressions. Mirza (1991) is critical of the lack of attention paid to the needs of ethnic minority communities in the National Health Service and Community Care Act 1990: 'Government failed to identify clearly the role of local authorities in ensuring that each aspect of their community care programme actively promoted equality or, at minimum, accounted for the impact of racial discrimination' (p. 123). As this is a major piece of legislation with regard to Social Services provision for disabled people, this criticism is a very telling one in relation to black people or people from ethnic minorities who are disabled and in need of services. It raises questions about the availability of ethnically sensitive service provision and perhaps identifies a barrier to the development of anti-racist practice.

In recent years there has been a notable, and very welcome, growth in literature addressing issues of anti-racist social work but sadly anti-racism in the context of social work with disabled people has yet to receive adequate attention. The dynamics of racism and disablism as a combination of oppressions remains a neglected area and one which clearly merits further research and the articulation of a coherent theory base. Stuart (1992) recognises the need for further work in this area and offers some useful pointers towards a more adequate theoretical understanding of the issues.

Oliver (1990) would also add gender as a further dimension of this under-researched area:

> In the absence of empirical data, there has also been little theorising on the effects of a combination of race, gender and disability on personal experience, though it has been suggested that concepts like 'multiple minority statuses' and 'multiple minority groups' might be a useful starting point for analysis (Deegan, 1985). [p.75]

None the less, despite the relative lack of material to inform our understanding of such multiple oppressions, the significance of such combinations can be readily appreciated and their implications for practice can at least begin to be addressed.

Towards anti-disablist practice

This chapter has outlined the development of a new approach to social work with disabled people that is quite radically different from traditional perspectives. Much of the change has stemmed from disabled people who have sought to rework the helper–helped relationship. The movement remains a 'consumer-led' one, but this is not to say that social workers do not have a major contribution to make. The remainder of this chapter is therefore a set of suggestions for taking steps towards an anti-discriminatory social work with disabled people. These are by no means the only steps, but will, I hope, none the less help social workers to engage with the issues and determine, in more detail, the route they wish to follow.

1. Disabled people are people first. This may seem straightforward but it is something which is not always recognised in interactions between social workers and disabled
   clients. The history of social work intervention with
   disabled people is not a particularly happy one (Sapey
   and Hewitt, 1991; and Morris, 1989). Much of the
   criticism has stemmed from the view that the focus tends
   to be on the disability rather than on the person (as per
   the medical model – see point 2 below). Anti-discriminatory practice must be based on seeing the person first,
   before the disability. As UPIAS put it: 'We look forward
   to the future – a world where physically-impaired people
   are truly people first, and last' (p. 46).
2. Social work with disabled people has for many years
   been dominated by the medical model. The social work
   task has been seen as a paramedical or ancillary task
   geared towards care-giving and rehabilitation. Preston–
   Shoot and Agass (1990) argue that a medicalised approach to social work has arisen, due to the failure of
   social work to develop its own theory base. The more
   critical approach to disability developed by Oliver,
   Finkelstein and so on is now capable of creating that
   theory base so that the medical model is not needed to
   'fill the gap'. Treating disabled people as if they were ill
   or necessarily in need of medical supervision is dehumanising and oppressive. Anti-discriminatory practice must
   therefore aim for a 'demedicalisation' of social work.
3. Traditional social work with disabled people is premised
   on an individual model of personal tragedy and efforts
   are geared towards the individual for his/her lack of
   functional ability. However, this has now been challenged by a social oppression model of disability which
   emphasises the personal, cultural, structural and envir-
   onmental barriers that prevent disabled people from
   participating fully in mainstream social, political and
   economic life. In fact, the individual model is seen as a
   further barrier to self-realisation as it translates issues of
   human rights intomatters of care and rehabilitation.
   Anti-discriminatory practice must therefore be based on
   a social, rather than an individual model of disability.

4. Following on from this, it needs to be recognised that the service disabled people's organisations are looking for is one based on rights rather than compassion. As Sapey and Hewitt (1991) put it:

> If we see disabled people as people in need rather than people whose rights to resources are being denied or rationed, then the concept of need can also become disabling. While it is necessary to review the language of legislation, it is more important to ensure that it is interpreted in a manner that will afford disabled people their rights. (pp. 42–3)

They go on to argue that there is a social work role in helping disabled people assert their own choices and thus move to a less dependent role. This can be a key part in the development of anti-disablist practice.

5. The dominance of disablist ideology which constructs disabled people as passive and pitiful victims of personal tragedy is reflected in and reinforced by the language used to refer to disabled people. It is therefore important to ensure that discriminatory and dehumanising language is avoided and discouraged. Depersonalising terms such as 'the disabled', 'the handicapped' or 'spastic' not only contribute to the oppression of disabled people but also legitimate such oppression by making it seem natural, 'normal' and a straightforward part of everyday life. A more sensitive and positive use of language is therefore called for.

6. Part of the discriminatory ideology of disablism is the tendency to see disabled people as those in need of aid, as opposed to 'normal' people who do not need such aid. This is an oppressive and divisive myth which isolates disabled people from the mainstream of society. By disguising the assistance all people rely on and the public resources which finance much of such assistance, the type of aiding required by people with an impairment appears to be 'special' and costly – and is therefore vulnerable to cutbacks and rationing and seen as a privilege rather than a right. It therefore needs to be remembered that *aiding is for all* and therefore the needs of impaired

people are different rather than a 'special case'. Social workers can play a part in drawing attention to this and thus contribute to 'destigmatising' disability.

7. Given that aiding is for all, we are all 'dependent' to some extent on assistance. The fact that such a reliance is exaggerated and overemphasised in the stereotype of disability is a further dimension of disablist ideology. It is therefore important that social work intervention has the effect of promoting independence as far as possible. There is a danger that an uncritical social work practice informed by received ideas will assume dependency to be the norm and thus run the risk of creating such dependency by establishing a 'self-fulfilling prophecy'. What is needed therefore is a practice based on partnership rather than paternalism.

8. A focus on independence is precisely the strategy of Centres for Integrated Living (CILs). These centres involve putting power and control into the hands of disabled people themselves. This is, of course, entirely consistent with anti-disablism, and a movement to be supported and encouraged. The development of anti-discriminatory practice will therefore be hindered by a traditional approach that sees the social work task in predominantly casework terms and therefore shies away from community involvement or wider-scale initiatives. CILs should not be seen as developments ripe for professional colonisation but nor should they be seen as a separate venture largely unconnected with the aims, values and interests of social workers.

9. The casework approach has also tended to produce an emphasis on practical tasks, a very pragmatic 'sorting out services and benefits approach'. It is no doubt partly due to to this that social work with disabled people has tended to be seen as a lower status branch of social work, often consigned to unqualified staff (Barclay Report, 1982). Social work with disabled people is a professional endeavour that requires commitment and a range of skills, including assessment, negotiation, advocacy, counselling and so on. Helping to overcome oppression is a skilled and demanding task and should

not be viewed as a subordinate, lower-status aspect of social work – as that would itself be a disablist assumption to make.

10. Perhaps the central concept in the development of anti-disablist practice is that of *empowerment*. Traditional approaches to disability continued to disempower people with an impairment, to deprive them of aspects of control over their own lives. They are disenfranchised by marginalisation, isolation and dehumanisation – at a personal level through prejudice and misdirected pity; and at a cultural level through negative stereotypes and values; at a structural level through a society dominated by capitalist notions of 'survival of the fittest' and charity for those who are 'handicapped' from competing. Empowerment amounts to working alongside disabled people to help overcome and challenge the oppression they experience. This involves counselling geared towards confidence-boosting and similar measures on the one hand, and advocacy and the promotion of citizenship on the other.

Social work has never been a static entity and is therefore no stranger to change and innovation. However, it must be recognised that the changes required to develop anti-disablist social work practice are, in many ways, major and radical. This does not mean it cannot be done; indeed it is already under way in some areas. But this is clearly a major challenge for social work and one to which I very much hope we are able to rise.

7

Other Sources of Oppression

Each of the preceding four chapters has concentrated on a major area of discrimination and oppression – gender, race, age and disability. However, it would be a mistake to assume that these are the only sources of oppression with which anti-discriminatory practice needs to concern itself.

There are many other forms and sources of oppression that have an impact on social work, and attention needs to be drawn to the wide range of issues not already incorporated in the four main areas covered so far. Arguably, each of the topics discussed in this chapter could justify a full chapter of its own. The fact that they 'share' a chapter is in no way an indication that they are unimportant or less relevant to social work. It is simply a matter of limitations on space – a text which did justice to such a range of topics would be vast indeed.

This chapter can therefore only expect to scratch the surface of these various areas. None the less, this is an important part of the process of developing anti-discriminatory practice as the first part of this process must be to recognise the existence of the form of oppression in question and thus begin to place it on the agenda. By raising some of the issues here, I hope I can contribute to raising levels of consciousness and thereby provide leads for interested readers to follow up and perhaps use as the basis of discussion and further learning.

Before proceeding to consider the various sources of oppression and thus broaden the analysis so far presented, I shall first outline some aspects of oppression which will help to cast light on the discussions that follow. This will set the scene for exploring the discrimination and oppression associated with sexual orientation, religion, language, nation or region, mental illness and mental impairment.

Aspects of oppression

In Chapter 2, oppression was defined as, amongst other things, 'the negative and demeaning exercise of power'. Similarly, Webster's *Third New International Dictionary* uses the phrase 'unjust or cruel exercise of authority or power' in its definition of oppression. Power and oppression are therefore closely linked.

In order to understand oppression as a dimension of the lives of social work clients (and potential clients) it is therefore necessary to be clear about the part played by power and how it operates. This is particularly important, as power is a unifying theme across the various subsections of this chapter – it is a concept that can be seen to apply in each of the topics covered. It links together what may otherwise appear to be a relatively unrelated series of issues. Hugman (1991) argues that: 'power is not an isolated element of social life, but one which interweaves occupational and organisational structures with the actions of professional, individually and collectively' (p. 38).

Where social workers, and indeed other welfare professionals, come into contact with clients, power is always on the agenda; it is 'an integral aspect of the daily working lives of professionals' (Hugman, 1991, p. 1). This has very much been the case in the preceding four chapters in terms of the power of men over women, white people over black, young over old, and able-bodied over disabled. In addition, we must recognise the power of social workers in terms of:

● knowledge and expertise;
● access to resources;
● statutory powers; and
● influence over individuals, agencies and so on.

Power is an aspect of the relationship between social workers and their clients – in addition to the social divisions that go to make up the social structure. This raise two sets of potential problems:

1. The social worker's power can be used in an oppressive way; that is, it can be abused (Thompson, 1991b).
2. The social worker may not be sufficiently sensitive to issues of power/powerlessness and oppression as they relate to clients in terms of their social location – gender, race, age and so on.

Anti-oppressive practice therefore needs to be very sensitive to issues of power, and not simply in relation to the four main areas of discrimination discussed so far. Power is a general feature of social work and is also specifically relevant to the other forms of discrimination outlined in this chapter.

Oppression is also significant in relation to identity. The traditional view of identity as a narrow, psychological issue is increasingly being challenged as sociological and political aspects of identity receive greater attention. And oppression is an important factor in understanding this wider view of identity formation. Hudson (1989) argues the need for a greater awareness of the structural aspects of identity. She argues that:

> The ways in which structural factors such as race, class and gender shape individual personality development and behaviour are considerable. It is important that these factors are acknowledged in the curriculum of social work training courses and in the assessments that social workers make of their clients. (p. 81)

Social workers have often been criticised for taking too narrow and individualistic an approach and thus failing to appreciate wider social patterns (Mills, 1970). For example, Dale and Foster (1986) are critical of psychodynamic approaches which do not recognise: 'that the problems faced by their individual female clients might have been more related to their positions in society than to their individual psyches' (p. 96, quoted in Rojek *et al.*, 1989, p. 2). Social workers who seek to develop anti-discriminatory practice need not only to move beyond the individual level to understand the social element, but also to appreciate how the social element has a major impact on the personal and subjective areas. Who I am is not just a matter of my unique and personal life-world, it is also a matter of my *social location* and to what extent I experience oppression.

The various forms of oppression – be it sexism, racism, disablism and so on, or, as we shall see below, heterosexism, sectarianism or internal colonialism and so on – can be seen to have an impact on identity in terms of:

● alienation, isolation, marginalisation;
● economic position and life-chances;
● confidence and self-esteem; and
● social expectations, career opportunities and so on.

The links between identity and oppression are significant, although an analysis that does justice to these issues is far beyond the scope of a more generalised text such as this. The basic linkages should none the less be borne in mind when considering the various sources of oppression discussed below.

The final aspect of oppression I wish to consider here is that of its complex, multi-faceted nature. This is to revisit and reaffirm the point made in Chapter 2: that there can be no simple or crude model of oppression and especially no spurious 'hierarchy of oppressions'. As we have noted, oppression is a dimension, or outcome, of a power relationship. Such relationships are, of course, diverse and many-sided, forming an intricate web of social patterns and inter-actions. To reduce this to a simplistic, unidimensional model of oppression as the evil or unenlightened behaviour and attitudes of certain social groups (men, white people and so on) is a form of crude 'reductionism'. It reduces a complex, empirically variable situation to the status of a monolithic, undifferentiated concept (Sibeon, 1991a; Cain and Yuval-Davies, 1990).

This complexity and variability is reflected in the diversity of sources of oppression outlined below and is also captured in this comment from Hudson (1989): 'The dynamics and effects of oppression are like a kaleidoscope where the configurations of, and relationships between, different forms of oppression are constantly moving and changing' (p. 93).

Having re-examined, and extended, our understanding of oppression, let us now move on and address, in turn, a number of additional sources of oppression, beginning with discrimination against gay men and lesbians.

Sexual orientation

The 1980s saw an increased awareness of issues of sexual orientation and the discriminatory and negative treatment of homosexuals. Such discrimination has increasingly been recognised as unjust and has, in some areas, been included in equal opportunities policies. The heightened awareness of such issues has been recognised in the coining of a new term in the anti-discriminatory vocabulary: 'heterosexism', which can be explained in the following terms:

> The term 'heterosexism' will be unfamiliar to many because it's fairly new. It has been coined, just as 'racism' and 'sexism' were coined, 'to describe an attitude of mind that categorises and then unjustly dismisses as inferior a whole group of fellow citizens'.
> (GLC, 1985)

The authors go on to stress the widespread and institutionalised nature of this form of discrimination:

> In the case of heterosexism, the oppression appears to assume that no one can naturally be homosexual but must be a failed or corrupted heterosexual.
>
> It is institutionalised in our laws, media, religions, and language, and in all too many family 'units'. Attempts to enforce heterosexuality are as much a violation of human rights as racism and sexism and must be challenged with equal determination. (ibid.)

There are strong parallels between heterosexism and other forms of discrimination (not least the applicability of PCS analysis). For example, there is a reliance on biological (or pseudo-biological) explanations of why homosexuality is not 'natural' and is therefore 'deviant' and to be discouraged. However, to argue that one form of sexuality is natural while another is not is a matter of ideological construction rather than biological explanation. It amounts, as Hoquenghem (1978) points out, to arguing that: 'Some of us are part of nature, and some not' (p. 48). The oppressive implications of this assumption are, of course, vast and so it is not too difficult to appreciate the negative impact of this aspect of heterosexism.

A further parallel is the alienation, marginalisation and destructive humour to which gay men and lesbians are subjected. A very negative and discriminatory attitude is even witnessed within the so-called caring professions. For example, Munro and McCulloch (1969), in a text written for social workers, comment that: 'Most lesbians are content to keep their homosexual inclinations hidden from general view and it is only the most psychopathic among them who make a show of their abnormality' (p. 157, quoted in Hart, 1980, pp. 46–7). One of the factors that can be seen to underlie heterosexism is a degree of paranoia. Plummer (1988) uses the term 'homophobia' to refer to the fear of homosexuality and the contempt for homosexuals which arises from it (GLC, 1985). Homophobia is therefore a key aspect of heterosexism.

Haselden (1991) discusses a similar theme and comments on the impact of AIDS on the gay community. He argues that the determination of gay people to be sexually active regard-less of AIDS is seen as self-destructive and self-indulgent. He then goes on to link this with the impression this gives to heterosexuals and the impact it has on them:

> At our most self-indulgent we show the futility of individual existence and inspire the hatred of a wider community, we remind people of their own mortality, we become perpetually discontent and rummage through the world looking for some purpose or meaning to our lives. (p. 20)

These comments add to Hoquenghem's view that: 'The problem is not so much homosexual desire as the fear of homosexuality' (1978, p. 35). Such fear and paranoia can lead to people having to conceal their sexual orientation and make a secret of their personal, intimate relationships or even deny them for fear of reprisal, ridicule or some other form of social sanction. For example, Webb (1989b) refers to a member of the Proud Old Lesbians group in London who allows her home help to assume she is heterosexual in order to avoid hostility.

Heterosexism can be seen as particularly problematic for older people or disabled people, as it is often assumed that they have no sexuality. The notion of homosexuality being applicable in the case of older or disabled people is therefore doubly oppressive for those prejudiced enough to subscribe to heterosexism – and therefore doubly oppressive for those so affected by this form of discrimination.

Discrimination against homosexual men and women can be seen to have two major sets of implications: one in relation to staff/service providers; and the other in relation to clients/ service users.

One common assumption which can have a profoundly discriminatory effect on staff is the false notion that homosexuals are a threat to children. It is commonly assumed by many people that homosexuals regard children as valid objects of sexual desire. This is reflected in, for example, the French use of the word *pédéraste*, which literally means 'lover of boys', to refer to homosexuals in general – and this is even confirmed in the dictionary definition (*Le Petit Robert*).

NALGO, the British trade union of national and local government officers, seeks to dispel this myth in its booklet *Gay Rights: NALGO Fighting Against Prejudice*:

> A homosexual person is no more likely than a heterosexual person to make sexual advances to clients, customers, fellow workers or the general public. There is no evidence at all that gay men or lesbians are more of a risk to children or adolescents. Indeed, there is evidence to the contrary. Gay workers have the same physical, mental and emotional characteristics as heterosexuals. Homosexuals are no more loyal, more selfish, more hardworking or more lazy. They differ only in being gay. That might have implications for their private lives but ought to make no difference to their working lives. (p. 4)

The irrational view of homosexuality as a threat is indicative of the paranoia which both reflects and reinforces heterosexist ideology.

This ideology is also apparent in some social work dealings with clients. As Webb (1989b) puts it: 'All the while social workers, home helps and so on at best assume clients are heterosexual and at worst make homophobic comments' (p. 21). An insensitive social work practice can therefore not only fail to play a part in tackling the oppression of heterosexism but can actually contribute significantly to such oppression. The development of anti-discriminatory practice must therefore be based on a greater understanding of homosexuality and heterosexism.

This is particularly the case in relation to childcare, in Britain at least, where the Children Act 1989 expects the self-esteem needs of gay young people to be addressed. Sone (1991) explains it as follows:

> [Social Services] departments must come out of the closet and place the needs of lesbian and gay young people firmly on the agenda. The potential for this revolution can be found in The Children Act. The guidance on family placements states that when leaving care 'the needs and concerns of gay young men must be recognised and approached sympathetically'. (p. 12)

Hopefully, of course, anti-discriminatory practice will amount to more than a sympathetic approach, as this has patronising and tokenistic connotations. However, as part of a broader-based commitment to fighting oppression, this is a worthwhile start.

Heterosexism is a deeply ingrained set of ideas and practices both within and outside social work. It is a significant and widespread form of oppression which merits inclusion on the anti-discriminatory practice agenda. I hope that in future it will receive the attention it deserves – far more attention than I have been able to give it here.

Religion

Religion is, of course, a major social institution which has profound effects on social organisation, politics, the economy, cultural norms and, not least, personal beliefs and values. The potency of religion is therefore immense.

The term 'religion' is frequently used in the singular as if it were a single, unified concept or force. However, we should not allow this to distract us from recognising the plurality of religion, the fact that we live in a multi-faith society. There exist a multiplicity of religions and, within the major religions, a number of 'subdivisions' or variations as, for example, in the Islamic faith. Such religious diversity is often closely linked with ethnic or racial groupings, although not exclusively so. Indeed, a sensitivity to, and awareness of, religious values and practices is a significant component of ethnically-sensitive practice as discussed in Chapter 4.

Religion is significant in relation to all three levels of the PCS model: *P* – one's religious beliefs (or lack of them) can be a fundamental part of one's identity and be a major guide to action on the basis of moral principles or required practices (for example, rituals). *C* – shared cultural norms and values can owe much to religion and can be enshrined in the particular religion's system of symbolic representations of reality. *S* – stratification systems can be based on religion (for example, caste) and, indeed, the links between religion and wider sociopolitical factors have been extensively explored (for example, Weber's study *The Protestant Ethic and the Spirit of Capitalism*, first published in 1904).

Religion can play a central part in the lives of social work clients at a number of levels and therefore needs to be taken into account in social work assessment, intervention, evaluation and policy planning.

Having clarified, to some extent, the need to take account of religious factors, let us now turn our attention to a particular dimension of religion and its relationship to discrimination and oppression. The issue I am referring to is that of sectarianism and I shall be using the example of Northern Ireland, drawing on the work of Brewer (1991). Brewer defines sectarianism as:

> actions, attitudes and practices determined by beliefs about religious difference, which results in them being invoked as the boundary marker to represent social stratification and conflict. (p. 101)

It is important to note that religion is not seen as the primary social difference but rather as indicative of other social or political differences. Brewer refers to a number of studies which 'highlight the importance of religion as a social marker through which conflict is articulated rather than as a source of conflict in its own right' (p. 101). Such conflicts include socioeconomic inequality between Protestants and Catholics and different political objectives (political union with the UK versus unity with the Republic of Ireland).

In many ways, sectarianism can be seen to parallel racism, and Brewer lists eight such parallels before going on to emphasise two of the main differences:

1. Sectarianism is based on discrimination relating to *stereotypical* assumptions (that is, generalisations about behaviour), whereas racism hinges on *phenotypical* assumptions (that is, generalisations about physical appearance).
2. It is possible to disguise, conceal or change one's religion and/or behaviour, whereas physical differences such as skin colour cannot be changed.

None the less, Brewer argues that some principles apply to both anti-racism and anti-sectarianism (and, indeed, perhaps more widely to anti-discriminatory practice in general). These are:

● equal treatment for people;
● protection from derogatory stereotypes, myths and abuse;
● protection of religious and cultural diversity; and
● equality of opportunity to society's rewards.

An understanding of sectarianism is clearly important for social workers in Northern Ireland, and Brewer's paper is helpful in drawing out some of the practice implications. However, we should note that, whilst Northern Ireland is a good example of sectarianism, the concept is, of course, far more widely applicable on a national and international basis than simply within the province.

Of course, sectarianism is not the only example of the interaction of religion and oppression or discrimination. Religion is a highly significant dimension of our existence at a number of levels and a wide variety of examples could be given of problems arising from conflicting religious ideologies. Space does not permit a detailed analysis of these but it is certainly worth exploring one particular area – the contradiction between some religious beliefs and some aspects of anti-discriminatory practice.

One example of this is the restriction on women and the concomitant inequalities enshrined in some religious doctrines. Similarly, Connolly (1991) discusses what she sees as dangerous aspects of religious fundamentalism. For example, she expresses concern about the creation of racially segregated schools and, later in the same article, she comments on:

'the further growth of religious bigotry, and racist bigotry sheltering under the name of religion' (p. 76). As with sectarianism, the issue here is not so much religion itself, but rather the social and political implications of certain aspects of certain religions.

This is a vast and complex area and I have only barely begun to scratch the surface in my treatment of the issues here. Much work remains to be done before our understanding of these matters even begins to approach a level of adequacy. It is important that social workers acknowledge the complexity and vastness of this dimension of social interaction and thus recognise the need to seek advice and guidance in dealing with such issues. It is not possible for social workers to be 'experts' in this area, given our current level of knowledge. None the less, this should not be used as an excuse for failing to address such issues to the best of our abilities. It is through making such attempts that much of the necessary learning will take place.

Language, nation and region

As with our discussion of religion above, the issues of language and nation – and, to a lesser extent, region – are very relevant to the subject matter of Chapter 4 in relation to ethnicity and racism. There are, of course, close links between factors associated with one's language, national or regional identity and ethnic groupings.

A key unifying concept in this area is that of *culture* – shared ways of seeing, thinking and doing. Cultural values and norms differ across regions and nations and, also within or across linguistic groups. Indeed, language is a central part of culture. As Carter and Aitchison (1986) comment:

> The character and vitality of a culture is to a large extent language dependent. Language helps to preserve traditions, shapes modes of perception, and profoundly influences patterns of social intercourse and behaviour. (p. 1)

They go on to quote Mandelbaum (1949, p. 162): 'No two languages are ever sufficiently similar to be considered as representing the same social reality' (ibid.). On this basis, the language or languages we speak (and, by implication, through which we conduct our social interactions) have a profound impact on the way in which we experience our existence – the medium through which we make sense of our world and construct our reality.

This will be very significant where the social worker is from a different linguistic background from the client or group with which he or she is working. This may be where languages of ethnic minority groups are involved, for example, Urdu or Gujerati, and the appropriate use of an interpreter is likely to be needed.

Making sure that members of ethnic minorities have the opportunity to communicate their needs, wishes and feelings is, of course, part and parcel of anti-racist practice. However, there are other cross-linguistic situations which are not so readily associated with racism – although *ethnocentrism* does tend to feature. I am referring to bilingual nations that exist; for example, Canada and Wales. To take Wales as an example, there are over half a million people within the principality who speak the Welsh language (1981 Census figures). Most of these people also speak English but it should be noted that for very many English is a 'second language'. For dealing with sensitive matters, perhaps of an emotional nature, communicating in one's first language is very much to be preferred.

This point has largely been recognised by CCETSW who have developed a policy on the Welsh language:

CCETSW has a responsibility to establish and maintain standards of education and training and to promote good and
effective practice. In Wales with its bilingual system of education
this reasonably requires CCETSW to ensure that Welsh medium
education and training is available and that English medium
education and training is culturally and linguistically sensitive.
(CCETSW, 1991a, p. 48)

And the policy goes on to recognise that a client has the basic
right to choose the language of interaction with the social
work agency. It is important, therefore, to ensure that
linguistic issues are addressed, particularly in bilingual communities. Failure to do so could add an extra layer of
oppression by forcing Welsh speakers (or indeed speakers of
any non-dominant language – the issue is not confined to
Wales) to communicate from a position of relative weakness.

Furthermore, to take no account of a client's first language
can be seen as devaluing that language and indeed the culture
of which it forms part and the personal identity of the client(s)
concerned. This is an example of 'ethnocentrism', the tendency to take one's own cultural or ethnic standpoint for granted
without reference to other perspectives, thus imposing one's
own definitions as the 'norm'.

One notable manifestation of ethnocentrism in this context
is to equate 'British' with 'English' as if Wales, Scotland and
Ireland were simply regions of England. This is captured in
Morgan's (1982) comment in which he refers to: 'that
notorious entry in the *Encyclopaedia Britannica* – in which
were encapsulated all the humiliation and patronising indif-
ference which helped to launch the modern nationalist movement in the principality – "for Wales, see England" ' (p. 3).
There are clear implications here for anti-discriminatory
social work practice. Social workers need to be sensitive to
the culture and values not only of black and ethnic minority
communities but also of national, regional and linguistic
groups. To ignore these factors is to ignore major aspects of
the client's experience, values and social location.

The concept of ethnocentrism is a useful one in so far as it
takes us beyond the individual level of personal prejudice and
emphasises the role of culture and thus the social dimension.
However, this in itself has limitations as it takes no account of

the structural level. One approach to these issues which does have a structural basis is that of Hechter (1975), who introduced the concept of 'internal colonialism'. Nairn (1986) describes it in the following terms:

> British capitalist development produced a set of of 'internal colonies' in its Celtic fringe, for basically the same reasons as it created external colonisation all over the globe. It is the contradictory nature of capitalist growth to do so. (p. 199)

Harris (1991), in a paper discussing anti-racist social work, draws parallels, between the oppression of black people and the historic treatment of the Welsh. He comments:

> Language is the main medium by means of which culture is transmitted. It is also the mechanism which enables the functions of conceiving, defining, refining and articulating ideas. Therefore if cultural hegemony is the objective, it is not surprising that bilingualism could not be tolerated either, as in the case of the Welsh the possession of that ability would have placed them in an advantageous position. The Welsh would have enjoyed the flexibility and facility of operating within and between two language mediums, while still retaining their cultural autonomy. In contrast the English ruling class would have been constrained, since being mono-lingual, they would have been unable to enter directly into the consciousness of the Welsh. Colonised people and immigrants are often encouraged by means of bribes or coercion to adopt the language of their oppressors. (pp. 138–9)

A key term here is 'cultural hegemony'. Anti-discriminatory social work should play no part in the maintenance of such dominance with its implied oppression of cultural or linguistic minorities.

The example given here has been that of Wales but the same issues can be seen to apply to a wider range of peoples in a wide variety of places in which social work is practised. Negative and derogatory stereotypes of Irish people is an example which springs readily to mind.

There is therefore a need for social workers to give due consideration to the issues of national, regional and linguistic identity as they apply in the locality in which they work. Without this there is a danger that an insensitive social work practice can contribute further to the oppression of 'cultural hegemony' rather than play a part in reducing the alienation and disempowerment it engenders.

Mental illness

Anti-discriminatory practice is not to be restricted to a particular client group or groups but there are specific issues which arise in relation to each such group. People who are defined as 'mentally ill' face areas of discrimination and oppression specifically as a result of being so labelled.

People who are deemed to be mentally disordered often encounter a negative response, even to the point of outright hostility, from the community at large. However, it is often the case that the response of professionals can also be experienced as oppressive. This is due, in no small part, to the tendency to view issues of mental disorder in terms of a medical model, that is to adopt a 'medicalised' approach. Such an approach has been criticised by many (for example, Laing, 1965; Heather, 1975; Ingleby 1981a; Thompson, 1991a) for its narrow and distorted perspective which presents moral, social and political matters as medical problems and therefore clearly located within the domain of the medical profession. Busfield (1986) describes Szasz's views on this issue in the following terms:

> The notion of mental illness is, Szasz claims, but a metaphor for what should, more accurately, be called 'problems in living', for except for the organic mental illnesses (those with identifiable physical causes) which would be better thought of as brain diseases, what is termed mental illness mystifies what is in fact a moral judgement, for the term illness suggests a scientific and objective assessment of sickness based on identifiable physical pathology. On the contrary it is a moral judgement and should be recognized as such. (p. 86)

Translating moral issues into medical ones has two implications which are particularly relevant to anti-discriminatory practice:

1. *Power*
   The 'medicalisation' of mental disorder gives considerable power to members of the medical profession and the administrative, technical and professional structures of which they form a part.
2. *Stereotypes*
   The classification system inherent in the medical model can be seen to have the effect of producing stereotypes of people said to be suffering from mental illness. It concentrates on generalities at the expense of specifics.

These are both key aspects of discrimination and oppression and so we need to look carefully at their impact on service users and systems of service delivery.

The power of the medical profession to define and control deviance is a long-established one which is not commonly challenged within welfare practice on a day-to-day basis. This power base and its influence on social work thinking and practice can act as a significant obstruction to the development of a social work of empowerment. This applies in a number of ways, for example:

1. As Conrad (1981) points out: 'medicalised definitions of deviance *remove responsibility* for behaviour from the individual' (p. 119). People diagnosed as mentally ill are disempowered and stigmatised by the application of such a label as their actions are deemed to be beyond their control. This then legitimises the use of external controls (medication, detention in hospital).
2. Banton *et al.* (1985) argue that medical discourse produces a cleavage between the individual's experience of pain or distress and the wider social context which underpins it. Thus the emphasis is on 'treating' individuals rather than tackling the underlying sources of distress:

   > Thus medicine is consumed instead of action being taken; questions surrounding the massive incidence of stress and disturbance in society are transformed into arguments over the adequacy of resources for 'treatment'. (p. 36)

This is a further example of 'blaming the victim' by reducing a complex web of social, moral, political and economic factors to a simple pathology 'within' the individual.

These two examples both relate to power and the individual but in different ways. In the first, the personal power of the individual is denied and in the second the effects of wider power structures are translated into individual pathology. In both cases the individual is disempowered. Similar issues apply to the process of stereotyping. Medicine claims to be an objective science and therefore seeks to establish clear and explicit diagnostic categories. And, of course, when categories are being applied to people, the danger of stereotyping is one to be wary of.

This applies particularly to the diagnostic label of 'schizophrenia' which is a much disputed concept. It has been criticised by many as a vague 'catch-all' which covers a broad range of problems. This lack of rigour is captured by the statistic that a person is two to three times more likely to be diagnosed as schizophrenic in the United States of America than in Britain (Miles, 1987).

Applying labels to people on the basis of a dubious scientific objectivity is a process which has distinctly oppressive connotations. There is a clear danger of setting up stereotypical expectations which have profoundly negative and discriminatory implications. It is evident, therefore, that an uncritical approach to mental health social work which adopts the tenets of the medical model is not conducive to anti-discriminatory practice. What is called for is an approach which is more attuned to the cultural and structural levels and does not stop short at the individual level.

The cultural level is important in terms of shared meanings and values – the context in which the supposedly 'schizophrenic' behaviour can be rendered intelligible (Laing and Esterson, 1970). That is, we cannot assume, as conventional psychiatry does, that 'mad' behaviour is meaningless and without foundation. An anti-discriminatory approach would be less dismissive and would be more attuned to R. D. Laing's:

long struggle to show that those labelled 'schizophrenic' are coherent in their agony – that their turns of phrase, silences, behaviour and hallucinations make a certain sense, given some dispassionate knowledge of the relationships within which they are located. (Ticktin, 1989, p. 4)

The structural level is also very relevant. Consider, for example, the links between gender and mental health (Brown and Harris, 1978) or race and mental health (Francis, 1991a, 1991b). But even beyond this, the medical model can itself be seen as a generalised vehicle of oppression. As White (1988) comments:

I see madness as a political/biological revolt against repressive normality, a system of fear and conformity where people are afraid to think and behave differently. Psychiatry is a way of terrorising people back into a normality where they won't revolt against an oppressive system of social and economic relationships. (p. 22)

Clearly this view raises a number of issues which merit much more attention than I am able to devote to them here. None the less, I hope my main point is clear, namely that the medical model with its individualist focus has a discriminatory and oppressive impact and is therefore not an adequate basis for anti-discriminatory practice.

Mental impairment

For many years issues of mental illness and mental impairment were dealt with together in policy and legislation under the generic title of 'Mental Health'. Now, however, they are increasingly being treated as separate entities, although some degree of overlap still remains.

One significant difference between the two sets of issues is, of course, that the biological basis of mental illness is disputed whilst the physiological basis of mental impairment is widely accepted. However, the fact that there is a physiological dimension should not be used as a basis for justifying a medically-orientated approach to this area of practice. Oliver's (1990) critique of the medicalisation of disability can also be seen to apply to mental impairment as the marginalisation and dehumanisation inherent in disablism are also applicable to people who have a mental impairment (for example, Down's Syndrome). Many of the points raised in Chapter 6 are therefore also very relevant here for it can equally be argued that any 'functional disability' engendered by the impairment is amplified and magnified by the social response which attaches negative stereotypes and marginalises yet another group of citizens from the mainstream of social life.

The social response has gone through various stages over the years forming four distinct models of mental impairment:

The threat to society model

This was a dominant view at the beginning of the century and was influenced by the eugenics movement who saw mentally impaired people as 'morally defective' and thus a threat to the social order. Thankfully, this view is no longer dominant but is none the less still evident in the attitudes of some people.

The medical model

The development of the National Health Service in Britain in the 1940s played a key part in helping the medical profession establish a dominant position and redefine the 'problem' as a medical one, thus requiring the development of a new medical specialism.

The subnormality model

In this model the focus is on educational achievement and the perceived limitations engendered by mental impairment. A key aspect of this model is the measurement of intelligence by means of IQ tests. As IQ is measured in relation to chronological age one implication of this model is that people with a mental impairment are seen as perpetual children: they are **sub**normal.

The special needs model

The focus here is on 'learning difficulties' and attempts are made to achieve the integration of people with a mental impairment into ordinary life as far as possible. However, the emphasis is on *special* needs and this, in itself, establishes barriers to full integration especially as the focus remains on the individual and his/her perceived inadequacies rather than on social organisation.

Although there is a broad chronological development from models 1 to 4 this can be misleading, as elements of earlier models persist and influence later models. However, what all these models have in common is a tendency to marginalise and disempower, to a greater or lesser extent, people with a mental impairment in much the same way as disablism does. Indeed, the discussion in Chapter 6, on 'the structure of aiding' is equally applicable in this context. We can question the appropriateness of providing services on an individualistic basis without taking account of the commonalities, of the status of people with a mental impairment as members of a disadvantaged social group whose rights can be affected by negative, demeaning and patronising social attitudes. What is needed, from an anti-discriminatory point of view, is an approach which:

> stresses the humanity of those affected and their right to a place in society an a fair share of resources, using a logic similar to that used to argue against racial and sexual prejudice. (Clements, 1987, p. 3)

The concept of 'normalisation' (Wolfensberger, 1972) has been very influential in seeking to reintegrate people with learning difficulties into mainstream society. However, the fact that attempts to 'normalise' are directed predominantly at those people excluded rather than the processes, structures or ideologies which promote such exclusion in the first place suggests a strong element of blaming the victim.

A further criticism of normalisation arises in relation to its conception of just what is normal. This is particularly the case in relation to members of ethnic minority communities. For example, Baxter *et al.* (1990) are critical of the texts used in assessment procedures:

> Such tests are based on the assumption that individuals will identify with images based on white middle-class lifestyles and

experiences. Racial stereotyping, inappropriate cultural approaches and language or communication difficulties further decrease the value of traditional assessments for black and ethnic minority children. (p. 23)

Despite these problems there does appear to be a growing movement away from a paternalistic 'looking after these poor people' approach towards a genuine aim of empowerment and maximum independence or, to use Phillipson's (1989) term 'interdependence'.

Once again, this brief analysis most certainly does not do justice to the complexity of the issues but I hope it has succeeded in its more modest aim of raising awareness of some of the elements involved in developing a truly anti-discriminatory practice. As with each of the topics discussed in this chapter, we have been able only to skim the surface of the areas concerned. The aim has been one of flagging up a range of issues which merit further study, debate and development as part of the struggle to achieve a social work practice and theory base premised on principles of anti-discrimination and anti-oppression.

8

Conclusion

Establishing a basis of equality of opportunity in service provision is no easy matter. The situation is made extremely complex by virtue of the number of forms of discrimination, the subtle and intricate ways they manifest themselves and the vested power interests which act as obstacles to change. Consequently, there can be no simple formula solutions which give a clear and straightforward path to follow.

The full development of anti-discriminatory practice must be a longer-term aim if more than lip-service is to be achieved. This does not mean that significant improvements and advances cannot be made in the short term. Indeed, the establishment of a strong edifice of anti-discriminatory policy and practice in the long term will depend on the firm foundations to be laid in the short term. The success of such a venture must depend ultimately on collective action and commitment. But each individual has a part to play in the major change from traditional approaches to social work to a form of practice based on principles of anti-discrimination and anti-oppression.

This book is intended as a guide for those who wish to play their part in this major change. But it must be recognised that it is only a guide; in itself it cannot produce anti-discriminatory practice. It can only make a contribution by:

- helping to develop the necessary knowledge base;
- stimulating debate, discussion and further study of the relevant issues;
- motivating readers to develop the skills, values and attitudes needed;

149

● encourage the creation of support groups and a collective approach; and
● act as an introduction, and bridge, to other more specialist texts on the subject.

To facilitate meeting these aims it would be helpful to restate some of the main themes of the book, by way of concluding summary, and to examine some of the issues affecting the way forward.

The main themes

There have been a number of recurring themes and it is perhaps worth commenting briefly on each of these in turn.

Power

Social work is a *political* activity; that is, it operates within the context of sets of power relations – the power of law and the state, the power inherent in social divisions such as class, race and gender, and the micro-level power of personal interactions. Also, many of the problems social workers tackle have their roots in the abuse of power – child abuse, for example.

PCS Analysis

Traditional social work relates primarily to the level of the individual with some limited recognition of the level of culture, values and shared meanings. Anti-discriminatory practice, by contrast, takes a much wider view – indeed a holistic perspective – which takes account of all *three* levels, the personal, cultural and structural and the interactions between them.

Ideology

An ideology is a set of ideas that both reflects and reinforces a set of power relations with which it is associated. For example, patriarchal ideology both reflects the powerful position of men in relation to women and, by promoting sexism, reinforces that power. Ideology acts as the 'glue' that binds together the three levels of the PCS model and, as such, has considerable discriminatory potential.

Oppression

Certain actions, attitudes and structures have the effect of oppressing particular individuals and groups – specifically those 'out-groups' which are discriminated against within the social structure. Often the oppression is unintended on the part of individuals but is none the less deeply ingrained in cultural patterns and institutional structures.

Empowerment

Traditional approaches to social work take little or no account of the oppression inherent in certain aspects of social organisation. They therefore see the social work task as one of *adjustment* to the 'natural order of things' rather than a contribution to the political struggle against oppression. Thus, the focus in anti-discriminatory practice is on *empowerment* rather than adjustment.

No middle road

Social work practice cannot avoid the question of discrimination and oppression. The actions of social workers and the policies of their agencies will have the effect of either (a) challenging and undermining, on a minor scale at least, the discrimination to which clients are subject; or (b) tacitly condoning and thus reinforcing such discrimination. There can be no middle road.

There are, of course, many other themes and issues that have arisen but I hope that the six outlined above encapsulate the main thrust of the anti-discriminatory philosophy expounded here. But how can these themes be integrated into day-to-day practice? How can they become an established part of social work? These are some of the issues I now wish to explore, in outline at least, and to focus on some of the dangers and obstacles that can stand in the way of developing a firm foundation of anti-discriminatory practice.

The way forward

Chapters 3 to 6 each ended with some guidance and suggestions concerning the implementation of principles of anti-discriminatory practice in relation to the particular area of discrimination being discussed. It is to be hoped that these points raised with regard to specific issues will encourage and stimulate practice developments in the fields of work concerned. However, we should supplement these specific aspects by considering more general suggestions concerning the translation of anti-oppressive theory into the reality of practice.

Again, I must be very selective as there is so much that can be said about these issues, so many debates yet to be worked through. I shall therefore restrict myself to ten particular comments – first, five positive steps I feel need to be taken, and then five dangers to be avoided.

Positive steps

1. Much of the discrimination inherent in social work can be seen to be unintentional – due to a lack of awareness rather than deliberate attempts to oppress. For this reason, *awareness training* has a major part to play. By bringing workers together in a training context, instances and issues of discrimination can be identified and levels of awareness can thus be raised. Greater awareness at the *P* level can begin to undermine, to some limited degree at least, discriminatory culture and ideology at the *C* level. Awareness training therefore begins the process of challenging and confronting discrimination. It also acts as a foundation for other forms and levels of training.

2. Awareness training provides a consciousness-raising role for individuals but its value can be multiplied by raised collective awareness and subsequent *collective action*. Examples of groups set up with this aim include: women's groups, race and culture groups, disability forums, equal opportunities monitoring groups. Recent years have seen a significant growth in the number and

influence of such groups. A collective response to examples of discrimination can have a much more potent effect than an individual response. In addition, each individual can act with greater confidence in the knowledge that there exists the backing of others within a collective anti-discriminatory project.

3. Sibeon (1991b) comments on anti-intellectual tendencies in social work which devalue theory and advocate a 'common-sense' approach to social work. This is a particularly dangerous approach as far as anti-discriminatory practice is concerned. 'Common sense' amounts, in fact, to a mixture of dominant ideologies – sexist, racist and soon. It is a collection of taken-for-granted assumptions which are likely to be discriminatory and oppressive in their content and impact. It is therefore essential that practice should be based on a clear and explicit theory base in order to be able to swim against the tide of dominant discriminatory assumptions. Anti-discriminatory social work therefore needs to be based on *applying theory to practice*.

4. In order to develop anti-oppressive practice we need to ensure that the issues and principles are seen as central – they are not an optional extra to be tagged on the end if time and resources permit. Equality of opportunity should be a central feature of all social work theory, policy and practice. It needs to be on the agenda for every service planning group, every working party, every course curriculum, every team philosophy and so on. Treating the subject as a separate, discrete area runs the risk of allowing it to become marginalised – a specialist subject for those who are interested, but not a mainstream issue. This is unacceptable, for, as we have seen, *good practice must be anti-discriminatory practice.*

5. Perhaps the most fundamental step towards anti-discriminatory practice that we can take is to become, and remain, *open and critical in relation to our own practice* (whether as direct practitioners, supervisors or educators). We need constantly to re-evaluate our practice and

examine it in relation to our anti-discriminatory aims. The prefix 'anti-' is very significant; it denotes fighting against a powerful and established ideology. If we become complacent by failing to check that we are carrying through an anti-oppressive stance, discriminatory ideologies can subtly re-establish themselves in our thoughts and actions.

Dangers

1. Anti-discriminatory practice challenges people's values and their taken-for-granted assumptions in constructing their own sense of reality. Such a challenge can prove very threatening and destabilising. If not handled sensitively, exposure to anti-discriminatory ideas and values can prove so alien and threatening as to arouse considerable resistance and barriers to change. Too strong and insistent an approach is likely to be counter-productive and raise obstacles rather than awareness; indeed, it could be argued that an insensitive and overzealous approach to 'converting' others is not only a disservice to anti-oppressive practice but also a form of oppression in itself. The focus needs to be on educating and convincing, not bullying.

2. The whole area of oppression and anti-discrimination is a complex and intricate field of study with many contentious and problematic aspects. It is a *political* matter and therefore subject to competing values and interpretations. Consequently, there can be no simple 'formula' solutions or easy answers. There are two interrelated dangers which arise from this: firstly, *reductionism*, the process of reducing a multi-faceted, multi-level set of issues to a simple, single-level entity (for example, reducing PCS to personal prejudice); and, secondly, *dogmatism*, translating an open and dynamic theoretical system into a closed and static belief system or dogma.

3. Anti-discriminatory practice is indeed a complex area with many dimensions, such as race, gender, age and so

on. One primary dimension which has received relatively little attention in this book is that of class. However, it has featured less here as it is more firmly established as a relevant factor in social work (due in no small part to the influence of the radical social work movement) and *not* because it is less important. A clear danger, therefore, is to fail to take account of the class dimension – the socioeconomic circumstances which (a) underpin and magnify other forms of oppression; and (b) act as a major source of oppression in their own right. The danger, therefore, is one of going from a situation (for example, in the 1970s) where class was seen as the primary, if not only, dimension of oppression, to a situation in which it is barely considered.

4. Class is part of the political underpinnings of anti-discriminatory practice and is also a key element in marxist theory which, in turn, is a central feature of radical social work. The influence of marxism has declined in recent years to be replaced, to a certain extent, by a New Right philosophy which seeks to 'roll back the state' by lessening the state's role in welfare provision. The resulting privatisation of welfare and its reliance on the profit motive are unlikely to provide fertile soil for the development of anti-oppressive practice. Although the crude marxism of the 'Case Con' radicalism of the 1960s offered a far from adequate basis for social work, the rejection of a socialist political philosophy seriously weakens the scope for developing anti-discriminatory practice.

5. A further danger to be identified is that of 'colluding with the rhetoric'. What this means is that some people may use the right language and may make the right gestures but without any underlying commitment to the values and principles of anti-discriminatory practice. They are just 'going through the motions', perhaps to avoid being branded as racist, sexist or whatever, or perhaps through confusion, ignorance or insecurity about how to practise in a genuinely anti-discriminatory way. This is a parti-

cularly worrying state of affairs as it gives the impression that equality of opportunity is being pursued when, in fact, inequalities are being maintained, condoned and reinforced.

There are, of course, many other dangers and many other positive steps, although I am not able to pursue these here. The points raised are intended not as a comprehensive overview but as a set of pointers to guide and inform further discussion and action.

Social work is traditionally seen as operating on a knife edge of care and control. The discussions in this book, and more widely within the anti-discriminatory movement, not only recognise the significance of this knife edge but also relate it to another 'knife edge' situation. I am referring to the thin line between oppression and empowerment. That line also cuts through the centre of social work: the actions of social workers (and their agencies) are crucial in determining whether oppression is increased and strengthened or, alternatively, challenged and undermined through the process of empowerment.

Anti-discriminatory practice seeks to ensure that empowerment is to the fore, in order to ensure that social work is a progressive force for social change and amelioration rather than a repressive arm of an uncaring state bureaucracy. The challenge is a major one but the rewards for success are high, as indeed are the costs of failure.

Bibliography

Abberley, P. (1987) 'The Concept of Oppression and the Development of a Social Theory of Disability', *Disability, Handicap and Society*, 2 (1).

Abbott, P. and Sapsford, R. (1988) 'The Body Politic, Health, Family and Society', Open University, Unit 11 of D211, *Social Problems and Social Welfare*.

Abercrombie, N. and Warde, A. (1988) *Contemporary British Society*, London, Polity.

Ahmad, B. (1990) *Black Perspectives in Social Work*, Birmingham, Ventura Press.

Ahmed, S. (1987) 'Racism in Social Work Assessment', in BASW Social Work and Racism Group (1987).

Ahmed, S. (1991) 'Developing Anti-Racist Social Work Education Practice', in CD Project Steering Group (1991).

Ahmed, S., Cheetham, J. and Small, J. (1986) *Social Work With Black People and Their Families*, London, Batsford.

Allen, I. (1990) *Care Managers and Care Management*, London, Policy Studies Institute/Joseph Rowntree Memorial Trust.

Allen, S. (1987) 'Gender, Race and Class in the 1980s', in Husband (1987).

Amos, V., Lewis, G., Mama, A. and Parmar, P. (1984) 'Many Voices, One Chant: Black Feminist Perspectives', *Feminist Review*,17.

Anderson, J. and Ricci, M. (eds) (1990) *Society and Social Science: A Reader*, Milton Keynes, Open University.

Ash, A. (1984) 'Father–Daughter Sexual Abuse: The Abuse of Paternal Authority', monograph, University College of North Wales.

Bailey, R. and Brake, N. (eds) (1975) *Radical Social Work*, London, Edward Arnold.

Bailey, R. and Brake, N. (1980) 'Contributions to a Radical Practice in Social Work', in Brake and Bailey (1980).

Banton, R., Clifford, P., Frosh, S., Lousada, J. and Rosenthall, J. (1985) *The Politics of Mental Health*, London, Macmillan.

Barclay Report, (1982) *Social Workers: Their Roles and Tasks*, London, Bedford Square Press.

Barker, M. (1981) *The New Racism: Conservatives and the Ideology of the Tribe*, London, Junction Books.

Barnes, C. (1991a) *Institutional Discrimination Against Disabled People: A Case for Legislation*, London, British Council of Organisations of Disabled People.

Barnes, C. (1991b) *Disabled People in Britain andDiscrimination: A Case For Anti-Discrimination Legislation*, London, Hurst and Co. in association with BCODP.

Barrett, M. (1980) *Women's Oppression Today*, London, Verso.

Barrett, M. and McIntosh, M. (1980) 'The Family Wage', in Whitelegg *et al.*, (1987).

BASW Social Work and Racism Group (1987) *Racism and Social Work Practice – Time For A Change*, Birmingham, BASW.

Baxter, C., Poonia, K., Ward, L. and Nadirshaw, J. (1990) *Double Discrimination*, London, King's Fund Centre.

Beagley, J. M. (1989) 'Gender Issues in Child Abuse, She Must Have Known What Was Happening', *Child Abuse Review*, 3 (2).

Beauvoir, S. de (1972) *The Second Sex*, Harmondsworth, Penguin.

Beauvoir, S. de (1977) *Old Age*, Harmondsworth, Penguin.

Beloff, M. S. (1976) *Sex Discrimination: The New Law*, London, Butterworth.

Berger, P. L. (1966) *Invitation To Sociology*, Harmondsworth, Penguin.

Berger, P. L. and Luckmann, T. (1967) *The Social Construction of Reality*, Harmondsworth, Penguin.

Bhat, A., Carr-Hill, R. and Ohri, S. (eds) (1988) *Britain's Black Population: A New Perspective*, Aldershot, Gower.

Bhavnani, K. and Coulson, M. (1986) 'Tranforming Socialist Feminism: the Challenge of Racism', *Feminist Review*, 2.

Board for Social Responsibility (1990) *Ageing*, London, Church House Publishing.

Borsay, A. (1986) 'Personal Trouble or Public Issue? Towards a Model of Policy for People with Physical and Mental Disabilities', *Disability, Handicap and Society*, 1 (2).

Boswell, D. M. and Wingrove, J. M. (eds) (1974) *The Handicapped Person in the Community*, London, Tavistock/Open University Press.

Bottomore, T. B. and Rubel, M. (eds) (1963) *Selected Writings in Sociology and Social Philosophy,* Harmondsworth, Penguin.

Brah, A. and Deem, R. (1986) 'Towards Anti-Sexist and Anti-Racist Schooling', *Critical Social Policy*, 16.

Brake, M. and Bailey, R. (eds) (1980) *Radical Social Work and Practice*, London, Edward Arnold.

Brearley, C. P. (1982) *Risk and Ageing,* London, Routledge & Kegan Paul.

Brechin, A., Liddiard, P. and Swain, J. (eds) (1981) *Handicap in a Social World*, London, Open University/Hodder & Stoughton.

Brenner, J. and Ramas, M. (1990) 'Rethinking Women's Oppression', in Lovell (1990).

Brewer, J. D. (1991) 'The Parallels Between Sectarianism and Racism: the Northern Ireland Experience', in CCETSW (1991b).

Brisenden, S. (1986) 'Independent Living and the Medical Model of Disability', *Disability, Handicap and Society*, 1 (2).

Brittan, A. and Maynard, M. (1984) *Sexism, Racism and Oppression*, Oxford, Basil Blackwell.

Bromley, D. and Longino, C. F. Jnr (1972) *White Racism and Black Americans*, Cambridge, Mass., Schenkman.

Brook, E. and Davis, A. (eds) (1985) *Women, The Family and Social Work*, London, Tavistock.

Brown, G. W. and Harris, T. (1978) *The Social Origins Of Depression*, London, Tavistock.

Bryan, B., Dadzie, S. and Scafe, S. (1985) *The Heart Of The Race*, London, Virago.

Bullock, A. and Stallybrass, O. (1977) *Dictionary Of Modern Thought,*, London, Fontana.

Burke, A. (1984) 'Racism and Mental Illness', *International Journal of Social Psychiatry*, 29 (1).

Burke, A. (1986) 'Social Work and Intervention in West Indian Psychiatric Disorder', in Coombe and Little (1986).

Busfield, J. (1986) *Managing Madness: Changing Ideas and Practice*, London, Hutchinson.

Butler, R. N. (1975) *Why Survive? Being Old in America*, New York, Harper & Row.

Bynoe, I., Oliver, M. and Barnes, C. (1991) *Equal Rights For Disabled People: The Case for a New Law*, London, Institute for Public Policy Research.

Bytheway, W. R. (1985) 'The Later Part of Life: A Study of the Concept of Old Age', Occasional Paper No. 10, School of Social Studies, University College, Swansea.

Bytheway, W. R. and Johnson, J. (1990) 'On Defining Ageism', *Critical Social Policy*, 29.

Cain, H. and Yuval-Davies, N. (1990) 'The "Equal Opportunities Community" and the Anti-Racist Struggle', *Critical Social Policy*, 29.

Cameron, E., Badger, F. and Evers, H. (1989) 'How the Services Categorise', *Community Care*, 25 May 1989.

Carby, H. V. (1982) 'White Woman Listen! Black Feminism and the Boundaries of Sisterhood', in CCCS (1982).

Carlen, P. and Worrall, A. (eds) (1987) *Gender, Crime and Justice*, Milton Keynes, Open University Press.

Carter, H. and Aitchison, J. (1986) 'Language Areas and Language Change in Wales: 1961–1981', in Hume and Pryce (1986).

Carter, P., Jeffs, T. and Smith, M. (1989) *Yearbook of Social Work and Social Welfare 1*, Milton Keynes, Open University Press.

Cartledge, S. and Ryan, J. (1983) *Sex and Love: New Thoughts on Old Contradictions*, London, Women's Press.

Carver, V. and Liddiard, P. (eds) (1978) *An Ageing Population*, Sevenoaks, Hodder & Stoughton.

CCCS (1982) *The Empire Strikes Back*, London, Hutchinson.

CCETSW (Central Council for Education and Training in Social Work) (1989) 'Requirements and Regulations for the Diploma in Social Work', Paper 30, London, CCETSW.

CCETSW (1991a) 'Rules and Requirements for the Diploma in Social Work, Paper 30, 2nd edn, London, CCETSW.

CCETSW (1991b) *One Small Step Towards Racial Justice*, London, CCETSW.

CD Project Steering Group (eds) (1991) *Setting the Context for Change*, London, CCETSW.

Cheetham, J. (ed.) (1981) *Social and Community Work in a Multi-Racial Society*, London, Harper & Row.

Chakrabarti, M. (1990) 'Radical Prejudice', Open University, Workbook 6, Part 1 of K254, *Working with Children and Young People*.

Clements, J. (1987) *Severe Learning Disability and Psychological Handicap*, Chichester, John Wiley.

Coates, D. (1990) 'Traditions of Thought and the Rise of Social Science in the United Kingdom', in Anderson and Ricci (1990).

Connelly, N. (1988) *Race and Change in Social Services Departments*, London, Policy Studies Institute.

Connolly, C. (1991) 'Washing our Linen: One Year of Women Against Fundamentalism', *Feminist Review*, 37.

Conrad, P. (1981) 'On the Medicalisation of Deviance and Social Control', in Ingleby (1981b).

Coombe, V. and Little, A. (eds) (1986) *Race and Social Work*, London, Tavistock.

Cooper, C. and Davidson, M. (1982) *High Pressure: Working Lives of Women Managers*, London, Fontana.

Cooper, D. (ed.) (1968) *The Dialectics of Liberation*, Harmondsworth, Penguin.

Cope, R. (1989) 'The Compulsory Detention of Afro-Caribbeans Under the Mental Health Act', *New Community*, 15 (3).

Corby, B. (1989) 'Alternative Theory Bases in Child Abuse' in Stainton Rogers *et al.* (1989).

Corrigan, P. (ed.) (1980) *Capitalism, State Formation and Marxist Theory*, London, Quartet.

Corrigan, P. and Leonard, P. (1978) *Social Work Practice Under Capitalism: A Marxist Approach*, London, Macmillan.

Coveney, L., Jackson, M., Jeffries, S., Kay, L. and Mahony P. (eds) (1984) *The Sexuality Papers: Male Sexuality and the Social Control of Women*, London, Hutchinson.

CPA (1990) *Community Life: A Code of Practice for Community Care*, London, Centre for Policy on Ageing.

Dale, J. and Foster, P. (1986) *Feminism and The Welfare State*, London, Routledge & Kegan Paul.

Davis, K. (1988) 'Issues in Disability: Integrated Living', Open University, Unit 19 of D211, *Social Problems and Social Welfare*.

Deegan, M. (1985) 'Multiple Minority Groups: A Case Study of Physically Disabled Women', in Deegan and Brooks (1985).

Deegan, M. and Brooks, N. (eds) (1985) *Women and Disability: The Double Handicap*, New Brunswick, Transaction Books.

Denney, D. (1983) 'Some Dominant Perspectives in the Literature Relating to Multi-Racial Social Work', *British Journal of Social Work*, 13.

DCDP (1985) 'Development of the Derbyshire Centre for Integrated Living', Chesterfield, Derbyshire Coalition of Disabled People.

Divine, D. (1990) 'Sharing the Struggle', *Social Work Today*, 22 November 1990.

Dominelli, L. (1986) 'Father–Daughter Incest: Patriarchy's Shameful Secret', *Critical Social Policy*, 16.

Dominelli, L. (1988) *Anti-Racist Social Work*, London, Macmillan.

Dominelli, L. (1989a) 'White Racism, Poor Practice', *Social Work Today*, 12 January 1989.

Dominelli, L. (1989b) 'An Uncaring Profession? An Examination of Racism in Social Work', *New Community*, 15 (3).

Dominelli, L. (1991) *Women and Community Action*, Birmingham, Venture Press.

Dominelli, L. and McLeod, E. (1989) *Feminist Social Work*, London, Macmillan.

Donnison, D. and Ungerson, C. (1982) *Housing and Social Policy*, Harmondsworth, Penguin.

Doyal, L. (1983) 'The Crippling Effects of Underdevelopment', in Shirley (1983).

Duncan, D. (1986) 'Eliminate the Negative', *Community Care*, 5 June 1986.

Ely, P. and Denney, D. (1987) *Social Work in a Multi-Racial Society*, Aldershot, Gower.

Engels, F. (1976) *The Origin of the Family, Private Property and the State*, London, Lawrence & Wishart (first published 1844).

EOC (1982) 'Caring for the Elderly and Handicapped: Community Care Policies and Women's Lives', Manchester, Equal Opportunities Commission.

EOC (1984) 'Carers and Services: A Comparison of Men and Women Caring for Dependent Elderly People', Manchester, Equal Opportunities Commission.

Esland, G. (1981) 'Language and Social Reality', Open University, Block 2, Part II of E263, *Language in Use*.

Fennell, G., Phillipson, C. and Evers, H. (1988) *The Sociology of Old Age*, Milton Keynes, Open University Press.

Fenton, S. (1987) *Ageing Minorities: Black People as They Grow Old in Britain*, London, Commission for Racial Equality.

Fernando, S. (1989) *Race and Culture in Psychiatry*, London, Tavistock/Routledge & Kegan Paul.

Ferns, P. (1987) 'The Dangerous Delusion', *Community Care*, 8 January 1987.

Festau, M. F. (1975) *The Male Machine*, New York, Bantam Books.

Finch, J. (1984) 'Community Care: Developing Non-Sexist Alternatives', *Critical Social Policy*, 9.

Finch, J. and Groves, D. (eds) (1983) *A Labour of Love*, London, Routledge &,Kegan Paul.

Fine, M. and Asch, A. (1985) 'Disabled Women: Sexism without the Pedestal', in Deegan and Brooks (1985).

Finkelstein, V. (1980) *Attitudes and Disabled People: Issues for Discussion*, New York, World Rehabilitation Fund.

Finkelstein, V. (1981a) 'Disability and the Helper/Helped Relationship', in Brechin *et al.*, (1981).

Finkelstein, V. (1981b) 'Disability and Professional Attitudes', Sevenoaks, NAIDEX Convention.

Finkelstein, V. (1991) 'Disability: An Administrative Challenge?',, in Oliver, M. (1991).

Firestone, S. (1972) *The Dialectic of Sex*, New York, Bantam Books.

Ford, J. and Sinclair, R. (1989) 'Women's Experience of Old Age', in Carter *et al.* (1989).

Foster-Carter, O. (1987) 'Ethnicity: The Fourth Burden of Black Women – Political Action', *Critical Social Policy*, 20.

Foucault, M. (1977) *Discipline and Punish: The Birth of the Prison*, London, Allen Lane.

Foucault, M. (1979) *The History of Sexuality, Vol. 1; An Introduction*, London, Allen Lane.

Francis, E. (1991a) 'Racism and Mental Health: Some Concerns for Social Work', in CD Project Steering Group (1991).

Francis, E. (1991b) 'Mental Health, Antiracism and Social Work Training' in CCETSW (1991b).

Freire, P. (1972) *Pedagogy of the Oppressed*, Harmondsworth, Penguin.

Friedan, B. (1968) *The Feminine Mystique*, Harmondsworth, Penguin.

Froggatt, A. (1990) *Family Work with Elderly People*, London, Macmillan.

George, M. (1991) 'Do It Yourself', *Community Care*, 9 May 1991.

Giddens, A. (1971) *Capitalism and Modern Social Theory*, Cambridge University Press.

Gilroy. P. (1987) *There Ain't No Black In The Union Jack*, London, Hutchinson.

GLC (1985) *Changing The World: A London Charter For Lesbian and Gay Rights*, Greater London Council.

Glendenning, F. (ed.) (1979) *Social Work With The Elderly*, Beth Johnstone Foundation/University of Keele.

Glendinning, C. (1987) 'Impoverishing Women', in Walker and Walker (1987).

Griffiths, R. (1988) *Community Care: Agenda for Action*, London, HMSO.

Gurnah, A. (1984) 'The Politics of Racism Awareness Training', *Critical Social Policy*, 11.

Haber, C. (1983) *Beyond Sixty-Five, the Dilemma of Old Age in America's Past*, Cambridge University Press.

Hall, S. (1980) 'Race, Articulation and Societies Structured in Dominance', in UNESCO (1980).

Hall, S. (1986) 'Managing Conflict, Producing Consent', Open University, Unit 21 of D102, *Social Sciences: A Foundation Course*.

Hall, S., Critcher, C., Jefferson, T., Clarke, J. and Roberts, B. (1978) *Policing the Crisis: Mugging, the State, Law and Order*, London, Macmillan.

Hallett, C. (1989a) 'The Gendered World of the Social Services Department', in Hallett (1989b).

Hallett, C. (ed.) (1989b) *Women and Social Services Departments*, London, Harvester Wheatsheaf.

Halmos, P. (1965) *The Faith of the Counsellors*, London, Constable.

Hamnett, C., McDowell, L. and Sarre, P. (eds) (1989) *The Changing Social Structure*, London, Sage.

Hanmer, J. and Saunders, S. (1984) *Well-Founded Fear: A Community Study of Violence on Women*, London, Hutchinson.

Hanmer, J. and Statham, D. (1988) *Women and Social Work*, London, Macmillan.

Harris, V. (1991) 'Values of Social Work in the Context of British Society in Conflict with Anti-Racism', in CD Project Steering Group (1991).

Hart, J. (1980) 'It's Just a Stage We're Going Through: The Sexual Politics of Casework', in Brake and Bailey (1980).

Haselden, R. (1991) 'Gay Abandon', *Guardian*, 7 September 1991.

Haynes, A. (1986) 'The Issue of Race in British Society', in Coombe and Little (1986).

Hearn, J. (1982) 'Radical Social Work – Contradictions, Limitations and Political Possibilities', *Critical Social Policy*, 4.

Hearn, J. (1987) *The Gender of Oppression, Men, Masculinity and the Critique of Marxism*, Brighton, Wheatsheaf.

Heather, N. (1975) *Radical Perspectives in Psychology*, London, Methuen.

Hechter, M. (1975) *Internal Colonialism: The Celtic Fringe in British National Development 1536–1966*, London, Routledge & Kegan Paul.

Henley, A. (1986) 'The Asian Community in Britain', in Coombe and Little (1986).

Heptinstall, D. (1986) 'The Black Perspective', *Community Care*, 31 July 1986.

Heraud, B. (1970) *Sociology and Social Work*, Oxford, Pergamon.

Hocquenghem, G. (1978) *Homosexual Desire*, London, Allison and Busby.

hooks, b. (1982) *Ain't I a Woman: Black Women and Feminism*, London, Pluto.

hooks, b. (1986) 'Sisterhood: Political Solidarity Between Women', *Feminist Review*, 23.

Howe, D. (1985) 'The Segregation of Women and Their Work in the Personal Social Services', *Critical Social Policy*,15.

Hudson, A. (1989) 'Changing Perspectives: Feminism, Gender and Social Work' in Langan and Lee (1989).

Hugman, R. (1991) *Power in Caring Professions*, London, Macmillan.

Hume, I. and Pryce, W. T. R. (eds) (1986) *The Welsh and Their Country*, Llandysul, Dyfed, Gomer.

Hunter, D. J. (ed.) (1988) *Bridging The Gap: Case Management and Advocacy for People with Physical Handicaps*, London, King's Fund.

Husband, C. (1980) 'Culture, Content and Practice: Racism in Social Work', in Brake and Bailey (1980).

Husband, C. (1986) 'Racism, Prejudice and Social Policy', in Coombe and Little (1986).

Husband, C. (ed.) (1987) *'Race' in Britain: Continuity and Change* (2nd edn), London, Hutchinson.

Husband, C. (1991) '"Race", Conflictual Politics, and Anti-Racist Social Work: Lessons from the Past for Action in the '90s', in CD Project Steering Group (1991).

Hutchinson-Reis, M. (1989)'"And for those of us who are black?" Black Politics in Social Work', in Langan and Lee (1989).

Ineichen, B. (1989) 'Afro-Caribbeans and The Incidence of Schizophrenia: A Review', *New Community*, 15 (3).

Ingleby, D. (1981a) 'Understanding "Mental Illness"', in Ingleby (1981b).

Ingleby, D. (1981b) *Critical Psychiatry: The Politics of Mental Health*, Harmondsworth, Penguin.

Jacobs, B. D. (1988) *Racism in Britain*, London, Christopher Helm.

Jeffries, S. (1984) '"Free From All Uninvited Touch of Man"': Women's Campaigns Around Sexuality, 1880–1914', in Coveney *et al.* (1984).

Jones, C. (1983) *State Social Work and the Working Class*, London, Macmillan.

Jones, C. and Novak T. (1980) 'The State and Social Policy', in Corrigan (1980).

Jones, H. (ed.) (1975) *Towards a New Social Work*, London, RKP.

Jong, G. de (1979) 'The Movement for Independent Living', in Brechin *et al.* (1981).

Joseph, G. (1981) 'The Incompatible Ménàge a Trois: Marxism, Feminism and Racism', in Sargent (1981).

Katz, J. (1978) *White Awareness*, University of Oklahoma Press.
Key, M. (1989) 'The Practice of Assessing Elders', in Stevenson (1989).
Kubisa, T. (1990) 'Care Manager: Rhetoric or Reality', in Allen (1990).
Kuhn, M. (1986) 'Social and Political Goals for an Ageing Society' in Phillipson *et al.*, (1986)
Kuhn, T. (1962) *The Structure of Scientific Revolutions*, University of Chicago Press.
Laing, R. D. (1965) *The Divided Self* , Harmondsworth, Penguin.
Laing, R. D. (1967) *The Politics of Experience and the Bird of Paradise*, Harmondsworth, Penguin.
Laing, R. D. (1971) *Self and Others*, Harmondsworth, Penguin.
Laing, R. D. (1975) *The Politics of the Family*, Harmondsworth, Penguin.
Laing, R. D. and Cooper, D. (1971) *Reason and Violence*, London, Tavistock.
Laing, R. D. and Esterson, A. (1970) *Sanity, Madness and the Family*, Harmondsworth, Penguin.
Langan, M. (1985) 'The Unitary Approach: a Feminist Critique', in Brook and Davis (1985).
Langan, M. and Day, L. (eds) (1992) *Women, Oppression and Social Work: Issues in Anti-discriminatory Practice*, London, Routledge & Kegan Paul.
Langan, M. and Lee, P. (eds) (1989) *Radical Social Work Today*, London, Unwin Hyman.
Lash, S. and Urry, J. (1987) *The End of Organised Capitalism*, Cambridge, Polity Press.
Leonard, P. (1966) *Sociology in Social Work*, London, Routledge & Kegan Paul.
Leonard, P. (1975) 'Towards a Paradigm for Radical Practice', in Bailey and Brake (1975).
Leonard, P. (1984) *Personality and Ideology: Towards a Materialist Understanding of the Individual*, London, Macmillan.
Leonard, P. (1989) 'Foreword', in Dominelli and McLeod (1989).
Lester, A. and Bindman, G. (1972) *Race and Law*, Harmondsworth, Penguin.
Loney, M., Bocock, R., Clarke, J., Cochrane, A., Graham, P. and Wilson, M. (eds) (1987) *The State or the Market*, London, Sage.
Lonsdale, S. (1990) *Women and Disability*, London, Macmillan.
Lonsdale, S. (1991) 'Out of Sight, Out of Mind', *Community Care*, 9 May 1991.

Lorde, A. *Sister Outsider*, New York, The Crossing Press.

Lovell, T. (ed.) (1990) *British Feminist Thought: A Reader*, Oxford, Basil Blackwell.

Lynes, T. (1974) 'Disabled Income', in Boswell and Wingrove (1974).

MacLeod, M. and Saraga, E. (1988) 'Challenging the Orthodoxy: Towards a Feminist Theory and Practice', *Feminist Review*, 28.

Mama, A. (1989a) 'Violence Against Black Women: Gender, Race and State Responses', *Feminist Review*, 23.

Mama, A. (1989b) *The Hidden Struggle*, London, LRHRU/Runny-mede Trust.

Mama, A. (1991) 'Race, Gender and Citizenship', paper presented at the Critical Social Policy 'Citizenship and Welfare' conference, London.

Mandelbaum, D. G. (ed.) (1949) *Selected Writings of Edward Sapir: A Study in Phonetic Symbolism*, Berkeley, Calif., University of California.

Manning, N. and Page, N. (eds) (1992) *Social Policy Review*, London, Social Policy Association.

Marshall, M. (1989) 'The Sound of Silence: Who Cares About the Quality of Social Work with Older People', in Rojek *et al.* (1989).

Marshall, M. (1990) *Social Work with Old People*, 2nd edn, London, Macmillan.

Marshall, V. W. (1986a) 'A Sociological Perspective on Aging and Dying', in Marshall (1986b).

Marshall, V. W. (1986b) *Later Life: The Social Psychology of Aging*, London, Sage.

Matthews, S. A. (1979) *The Social World of Old Women*, London, Sage.

Mayes, P. (1986) *Gender*, London, Longman.

Mays, N. (1983) 'Elderly South Asians in Britain: A Survey of Relevant Literature and Themes for Future Research', *Ageing and Society*, 3 (1).

McDowell, L. (1989) 'Gender Divisions', in Hamnett *et al.* (1989).

Mercer, K. (1984) 'Black Communities' Experience of Psychiatric Services', *International Journal of Social Psychiatry*, 30 (1/2).

Midwinter, E. (1990) 'An Ageing World: The Equivocal Response', *Ageing and Society*, 10.

Miles, A. (1987) *The Mentally Ill in Contemporary Society*, Oxford, Basil Blackwell.

Miles, R. (1989) *Racism*, London, Routledge & Kegan Paul.

Miles, R. and Solomos, J. (1987) 'Migration and the State in Britain: A Historical Overview', in Husband (1987).

Miller, E. J. and Gwynne, G. V. (1972) *A Life Apart*, London, Tavistock.
Millett, K. (1971) *Sexual Politics*, London, Rupert Hart-Davis.
Milligan, D. (1975) 'Homosexuality: Sexual Needs and Social Problems', in Bailey and Brake (1975).
Mills, C. W. (1970) *The Sociological Imagination*, Harmondsworth, Penguin.
Mirza, K. (1991) 'Waiting for Guidance', in CCETSW (1991b).
Morgan, K.O. (1982) *Rebirth of a Nation: Wales 1880–1980*, Oxford University Press/University of Wales Press.
Morris, J. (1989) 'Women Confronting Disability', *Community Care*, 29 June 1989.
Morris, J. (1991) *Pride Against Prejudice*, London, Women's Press.
Munro, A. and McCulloch, W. (1969) *Psychiatry for Social Workers*, Oxford, Pergamon Press.
Nairn, T. (1986) 'Culture and Politics in Wales', in Hume and Pryce (1986).
Nelson, A. (1990) 'Equal Opportunities: Dilemmas, Contradictions, White Men and Class', *Critical Social Policy*, 28.
Norman, A. (1980) *Rights and Risk*, London, Centre for Policy on Ageing.
Norman, A. (1985) *Triple Jeopardy: Growing Old in a Second Homeland*, London, Centre for Policy on Ageing.
Norman, A. (1987) 'Overcoming an Old Prejudice', *Community Care*, 29 January 1987.
Oakley, A. (1974) *The Sociology of Housework*, London, Pantheon.
Oliver, M. (1983) *Social Work with Disabled People*, London, Macmillan.
Oliver, M. (1984) 'The Politics of Disability', *Critical Social Policy*, 11.
Oliver, M. (1986) 'Social Policy and Disability: Some Theoretical Issues', *Disability, Handicap and Society*, 1 (1).
Oliver, M. (1987) 'From Strength to Strength', *Community Care*, 19 February 1987.
Oliver, M. (1989a) 'The Social Model of Disability', in Carter *et al.* (1989).
Oliver, M. (1989b) 'Social Work with Disabled People', *Social Work Today*, 6 April 1989.
Oliver, M. (1989c) Book Review of Hunter (1988) in *Disability, Handicap and Society*, 4(1).
Oliver, M. (1990) *The Politics of Disablement*, London, Macmillan.
Oliver, M. (ed.) (1991) *Social Work, Disabled People and Disabling Environments*, London, Jessica Kingsley.

Ong, B. N. (1985) 'The Paradox of "Wonderful Children": The Case of Child Abuse', *Early Childhood Development and Care*, 21.

Pannick, D (1985) *Sex Discrimination Law*, Oxford, Clarendon Press.

Parmar, P. (1982) 'Gender, Race and Class: Asian Women in Resistance', in CCCS (1982).

Parton, C. and Parton, N. (1989) 'Women, the Family and Child Protection', *Critical Social Policy*, 24.

Pascall, G. (1986) *Social Policy: A Feminist Analysis*, London, Tavistock.

Peace, S. (1986) 'The Forgotten Female: Social Policy and Older Women', in Phillipson and Walker (1986).

Pearson, G. (1975a) 'The Politics of Uncertainty: A Study in the Socialization of the Social Worker', in Jones (1975).

Pearson, G. (1975b) *The Deviant Imagination*, London, Macmillan.

Phillipson, C. (1982) *Capitalism and the Construction of Old Age*, London, Macmillan.

Phillipson, C. (1989) 'Challenging Dependency: Towards a New Social Work with Older People', in Langan and Lee (1989).

Phillipson, C., Bernard, M. and Strang, P. (eds) (1986) *Dependency and Interdependency in Later Life*, London, Croom Helm.

Phillipson, C. and Walker, A. (1986) *Ageing and Social Policy: A Critical Assessment*, Aldershot, Gower.

Philpot, T. (ed.) (1987) *On Second Thoughts*, London, Community Care/Reed Business Publishing.

Pierson, J. (1987) 'Keeping Faith', in Philpot (1987).

Pilkington, A. (1984) *Race Relations*, Slough, University Tutorial Press.

Pitt, B. (1982) *Psychogeriatrics: An Introduction to the Psychiatry of Old Age*, 2nd edn, Edinburgh, Churchill Livingstone.

Plummer, K. (1988) 'Masculinity, Homophobia and Sexuality', Open University, Unit 8 of D211, *Social Problems and Social Welfare*.

Polenberg, R. (1980) *One Nation Divisible*, Harmondsworth, Penguin.

Pond, C. (1989) 'The Changing Distribution of Income, Wealth and Poverty', in Hamnett *et al.* (1989).

Preston-Shoot, M. and Agass, D. (1990) *Making Sense of Social Work: Psychodynamics, Systems and Practice*, London, Macmillan.

Pritchard, C. and Taylor, R. (1978) *Social Work: Reform or Revolution?*, London, Routledge & Kegan Paul.

Pulling, J. (1987) *The Caring Trap*, London, Fontana.

Qureshi, H. and Walker, A. (1986) 'Caring for Elderly People: the Family and The State', in Phillipson and Walker (1986).

Rack, P. (1982) *Race, Culture and Mental Disorder*, London, Tavistock.

Ramazanoglu, C. (1989) *Feminism and the Contradictions of Oppression*, London, Routledge & Kegan Paul.

Rex, J. (1986) *Race and Ethnicity*, Milton Keynes, Open University Press.

Righton, P. (1990) 'Orientating Ourselves', Open University, Prologue to K254, *Working with Children and Young People*.

Rojek, C., Peacock, G. and Collins, S. (1988) *Social Work and Received Ideas*, London, Routledge & Kegan Paul.

Rojek, C., Peacock, G. and Collins, S. (eds) (1989) *The Haunt of Misery: Critical Essays in Social Work and Helping*, London, Routledge & Kegan Paul.

Rooney, B. (1980) 'Active Mistakes – A Grass Roots Report', *Multi-Racial Social Work*, 1.

Rooney, B. (1987) *Racism and Resistance to Change*, Liverpool, Merseyside Area Profile Group.

Roys, P. (1988) 'Social Services' in Bhat *et al.* (1988).

Rowbotham, S. (1973) *Woman's Consciousness, Man's World*, Harmondsworth, Penguin.

Rush, F. (1981) *The Best Kept Secret*, Englewood Cliffs, NJ, Prentice Hall.

Ryan, W. (1971) *Blaming the Victim: Ideology Serves the Establishment*, London, Pantheon.

Sapey B. and Hewitt N. (1991) 'The Changing Context of Social Work Practice', in Oliver (1991).

Sargent, L. (ed.) (1981) *The Unhappy Marriage of Marxism and Feminism: A Debate on Class and Patriarchy*, London, Pluto.

Sartre, J.-P. (1969) 'Itinerary of a Thought' (interview), *New Left Review*, 58.

Sartre, J.-P. (1975) *Critique of Dialectical Reason*, London, Verso.

Sennett, R. (1977) *The Fall of Public Man*, Cambridge University Press.

Shah, N. (1989) 'It's Up to You, Sisters: Black Women and Radical Social Work', in Langan and Lee (1989).

Shearer, A. (1981) *Disability: Whose Handicap?*, Oxford, Basil Blackwell.

Shirley, O. (ed.) (1983) *A Cry for Health: Poverty and Disability in the Third World*, Frome, Third World Group and ARHTAG.

Sibeon, R. (1991a) 'Emancipatory Theories, Policies and Practices in a Welfare Profession: An Anti-Reductionist Perspective on Social Work Politics', paper presented at the British Sociological Association Annual Conference, Manchester.

Sibeon, R. (1991b) *Towards A New Sociology of Social Work*, Aldershot, Avebury/Gower.

Simpkin, J. (1981) 'Financial Provision for Disabled Families', in Brechin *et al.* (1981).

Simpkin, M. (1989) 'Radical Social Work: Lessons for the 1990s', in Carter *et al.* (1989).

Sivanandan, A. (1991) 'Black Struggles Against Racism', in CD Project Steering Group (1991).

Small, J. (1989) 'Towards a Black Perspective in Social Work: A Transcultural Exploration', in Langan and Lee (1989).

Solomos, J. (1989) *Race and Racism in Contemporary Britain*, London, Macmillan.

Sone, A. (1991) 'Outward Bound' *Community Care*, 8 August 1991.

Sontag, S. (1978) 'The Double Standard of Ageing', in Carver and Liddiard (1978).

SSI (Social Services Inspectorate) (1991) *Women in Social Services: A Neglected Resource*, London, HMSO.

Stainton Rogers, W., Hevey, D. and Ash, E. (eds) (1989) *Child Abuse and Neglect: Facing the Challenge*, London, Batsford.

Stevenson, O. (1989) *Age and Vulnerability: A Guide to Better Care*, London, Edward Arnold.

Storkey, E. (1991) 'Race, Ethnicity and Gender', Open University, Unit 8 of D103, *Society and Social Science*.

Stuart, O. (1992) 'Double Oppression: An Appropriate Starting Point?', *Disability, Handicap and Society*, 7 (2).

Sullivan, M. (1987) *Sociology and Social Welfare*, London, George Allen & Unwin.

Thompson, N. (1989) 'Understanding Their Past and Family Life', *Community Care*, 25 May 1989.

Thompson, N. (1991a) 'The Legacy of Laing: A Critique of the Medical Model in Social Work and Social Care', *Social Science Teacher*, 20 (2).

Thompson, N. (1991b) *Crisis Intervention Revisited*, Birmingham, Pepar.

Thompson, N. (1992a) *Existentialism and Social Work*, Aldershot, Avebury.

Thompson, N. (1992b) 'Age and Citizenship', *Elders: Care and Practice*, 1 (1).

Ticktin, S. (1989) 'Obituary: R. D. Laing', *Asylum,* 4 (1).

Tolson, A. (1977) *The Limits of Masculinity,* London, Tavistock.

Townsend, P. (1981) 'The Structured Dependency of the Elderly: A Creation of Social Policy in the Twentieth Century', *Ageing and Society,* 1 (1).

Townsend, P. (1986) 'Ageism and Social Policy', in Phillipson and Walker (1986).

Townsend, P. and Davidson, N. (1982) *Inequalities in Health,* Harmondsworth, Penguin.

UNESCO (1980) *Sociological Theories: Race and Colonialism,*Paris, UNESCO.

Ungerson, C. (ed.) (1985) *Women and Social Policy,*London, Macmillan.

UPIAS (Union of the Physically Impaired Against Segregation) (1976) *Fundamental Principles of Disability,*·London, UPIAS.

UPIAS (1980) 'Disability Challenged', *The Bulletin on Social Policy,* 10.

Van den Bergh, N. and Cooper, L. B. (eds) (1986) *Feminist Visions for Social Work,* Washington DC, National Association of Social Social Workers.

Victor, C. (1987) *Old Age in Modern Society,* London, Croom Helm.

Walby, S. (1990) *Theorizing Patriarchy,* Oxford, Basil Blackwell.

Walker, A. (1981) 'Towards a Political Economy of Old Age', *Ageing and Society,* 1 (1).

Walker, A. (1986) 'The Politics of Ageing in Britain', in Phillipson *et al.* (1986).

Walker, A. (1987) 'The Social Construction of Dependency in Old Age', in Loney *et al.* (1987).

Walker, A. and Walker, C. (eds) (1987) *The Growing Divide,* London, CPAG.

Webb, S. (1989a) 'Dispelling the Myths of Disability with Awareness', *Social Work Today,* 6 April 1989.

Webb, S. (1989b) 'Old Lesbians: Out and Proud', *Social Work Today,* 4 April 1989.

Weber, M. (1930) *The Protestant Ethic and the Spirit of Capitalism,* London, George Allen & Unwin.

Weber, M. (1947) *The Theory of Social and Economic Organization,* New York, Free Press.

Weeks, J. (1986) *Sexuality,* London, Tavistock.

White, D. (1988) 'Madness and Psychiatry', *Asylum,* 3 (2).

Whitehouse, P. (1986) 'Race and the Criminal Justice System' in Coombe and Little (1986).

Whitelegg, E., Arnot, M., Bartels, E., Beechey, V., Birke, L., Himmelweit, S., Leonard, D., Ruehl, S. and Speakman, M. A. (eds) (1987) *The Changing Experience of Women*, Oxford, Basil Blackwell.

Whyte, A. (1989) 'The Long Route to Hospital', *Community Care*, 23 September 1989.

Williams. F. (1987) 'Racism and the Discipline of Social Policy: A Critique of Welfare Theory', *Critical Social Policy*, 20.

Williams, F. (1989) *Social Policy: A Critical Introduction*, London, Polity.

Williams. F. (1991) 'Citizenship, Social Policy and Theory', paper presented at the Critical Social Policy 'Citizenship and Welfare' conference, London.

Williams, F. (1992) 'Somewhere Over the Rainbow: Universality and Diversity in Social Policy', in Manning and Page (1992).

Williamson, J. (1979) 'Interprofessional Work with the Elderly' in Glendenning (1979).

Wilson, E. (1980) 'Feminism and Social Policy', in Brake and Bailey (1980).

Wolfensberger, W. (1972) *The Principle of Normalization in Human Services*, Toronto, National Institute on Mental Retardation.

Woolfe, S. and Malahleka, B. (1990) 'The Obstacle Race: The Findings of the BASW Report on an Action Research Project into Ethnically Sensitive Social Work', Birmingham, BASW.

World Health Organization (1980) *International Classification of Impairments, Disabilities and Handicaps: A Manual Relating to the Consequences of Disease*, Geneva, World Health Organization.

Zacune, C. (1991) 'Alternative Families for Black Children and Social Work Practice', Occasional Paper No.1, University of Keele.

Index